# THE MOST WIDELY PRAISED CAREER GUIDEBOOK IN YEARS!

"A lively and occasionally inspirational guide to maximizing opportunities . . . Scheele shares fresh ideas openly and unpretentiously, and quickly enlists the reader's trust."

*Los Angeles Times*

"A REFRESHING AND VERY HUMAN AP-PROACH TO SUCCESS."

*Publishers Weekly*

"THE MOST IMPORTANT BOOK IN CAREER DEVELOPMENT IN THE LAST TEN YEARS . . . SCHEELE'S SIX CRITICAL CAREER COMPE-TENCES WILL BECOME A STANDARD REFER-ENCE POINT FOR FUTURE DISCUSSIONS OF CAREER DEVELOPMENT."

Robert Ginn, Director Career Counseling
Harvard University

Also by Adele Scheele, Ph.D.
*Published by Ballantine Books:*

MAKING COLLEGE PAY OFF

# SKILLS FOR SUCCESS

## A Guide to the Top for Men and Women

Adele M. Scheele, Ph.D.

26391

BALLANTINE BOOKS • NEW YORK

To D. Sam,
for his constant and demonstrated love

# Contents

# Introduction

A young college graduate had found a job as secretary for a small five-man environmental planning firm. Five months later, she called me in despair over her duties—operating a copying machine, taking dictation, typing, and filing. Her only choice, she thought, was to quit and go back to school for an M.B.A. Was that a good idea?

I had no doubt that going back to school would be good for her. But even though she could apply immediately, she still would have to wait for four months for the new program to start. I suggested that we work on her job in the interim. Since she would be leaving soon anyway, she could take some risks to change her situation and increase her responsibilities by inventing new strategies and demonstrating her competence and intelligence, no holds barred. She agreed.

I had her tell me which of her activities or tasks she liked best. She could think of only one job that she liked; it was her first task early in the morning, after which everything seemed to go downhill. She read the daily national newspapers for stories of interest, then clipped them and laid them on the planners' desks. The best ninety minutes of her day were over before her first coffee break.

I told her that she was throwing away a good opportunity to advance herself. I advised her to change her approach, to dramatize the importance of her role in this task. I suggested that she hold on to the clippings and keep a weekly folder for each of the five planners. Then, at the regular Monday meeting, she would make a presentation on media coverage of planning issues. I stressed the importance of doing some homework. She had to think about her reasons for clipping a certain article, and act on them, by calling the people and organizations cited in the articles for more information about contracts, about the consequences of new regulations, about the competition in a particular market, or about the possibilities for joining a project, and so on.

Then she was to rehearse her delivery of the information she had, along with her suggestions. She was to present herself as an associate would, rather than as a secretary—two very different roles. After two meetings her employers asked her to write a project proposal, and two weeks later she held a newly created position as proposal writer.

Notice that I didn't suggest she learn any new technical skills or that she confront her group for not using her effectively. Instead, I urged her to formalize a routine task that she already liked to do, and to give it more importance—to present what she knew in a way that would command attention. She had, in fact, gathered a considerable amount of information, but she didn't know how to share it in the most valuable way. When she demonstrated an understanding of the firm's business, and pointed out new ventures of growth, she became a visible staff member. She could change how her employers saw her by changing how she behaved. The demonstration of intelligence and enthusiasm can create a job; before my client tried this new method of presentation, there was no position for a proposal writer. She couldn't have gotten it if she had asked.

The story is far from over. What to do as proposal writer? I suggested that she find out by investigating or by working on a proposal jointly with some other firm. If she could get to one group, then by the time she contacted the second, she'd have some information and/or people to share. She agreed to try. At the first meeting with the first company, she was pirated away. They were so impressed with her that they made her an immediate and better offer as a research analyst. She took it.

In four months she called again. She had gotten into the M.B.A. program, but she didn't want to leave her job. How to solve the dilemma? Do both. She argued that it was impossible to switch from the daytime program to the more popular one at night. I proposed that she go directly to the dean in charge of the night division and explain her situation. She was to emphasize her commitment (after all, she was already enrolled in the daytime program) and her enthusiasm. She should tell him how important the new job was to her, how much the degree would benefit her, and also point out the ways in which she could bring her company into the program as a resource for the students. I knew that there would be room in the program for another person, as inevitably someone drops out, and that when confronted with a list of faceless names, the dean would be most likely to choose the one name that had a personality attached to it. And that's exactly what happened.

A vice-president in charge of planning of a large California corporation confided to me that he was in stiff competition wth the other three corporate officers for the management of a new company soon to be acquired. My client thought that he was the most qualified to take control of the new service and personally was eager to extend his own expertise. But he had not had much contact with the president in recent weeks and was concerned that his invisibility had lost him his chance to get the desired position. He needed to reestablish his standing with the president.

I suggested some strategic planning first—an essential for any officer, but especially for a director of planning. How did the president usually make his decisions? Fast, within five minutes or so, he reported. My client would have to illustrate his qualifications in a comprehensive and objective way, and he would have little time to prove his point. We designed a graph that showed the responsibilities and time commitment of each of the four vice-presidents and the relative availability of each man for an added responsiblity. The graph clearly indicated that my client was the most appropriate choice for the job in question, since his efficient and competent work in his present capacity left him more time to take on another major task. The other vice-presidents were overcommitted.

We rehearsed how he would present his conclusions and, of course, himself. Simply stating his qualifications to the president would not do; the president already knew them and would react badly to a litany of accomplishments. Therefore, the best way to prove how capable and ready he was would be to demonstrate it. After all, he was in charge of planning and should exhibit his trade—problem-solving and future planning. He should be reflective, thorough, concerned, informed, and strong. Taking exactly six minutes to hear him out, the president directed him to assume management of the new company.

These successes only sound simple. Behind them lie the moves or strategies that go beyond the technical competence of either proposal writing or corporate planning. There's no magic, but there are a set of critical competences for successful careering that have been invisible for too long. I have identified them and described them in detail for you in the following chapters. They will work for you if you will work for them.

You will no doubt react to these skills in two ways. First, they should confirm much of what you already have been doing or at least know, from your own and others' experiences. And like all good theory, this should stimulate you to try more and different approaches in shaping what you want to do and therefore be. As you read these accounts and this theory, let me be your career coach.

# ☐ PART I

# CHAPTER ONE

# Realizing Reality: The Sustainers Versus the Achievers

*It is not enough to have great qualities:*
*We should also have the management of them.*
—LA ROCHEFOUCAULD

The world of working people divides into two distinct and telling categories, *Sustainers* and *Achievers*. These categories reflect our beliefs about how we should perform on the job. In this book I explain the differences between them, and show how we can all grow in our careers, enhancing our lives with the rewards that come from an active involvement in everything that we do.

## The Sustainers

The *Sustainers* are most of us who do our jobs well and derive our job satisfaction from doing just that. According to a Department of Labor study, doing our jobs well is more important to most of us than any other reward from work. In fact, most of us Sustainers spend about 70 percent of our working lives doing our jobs well and 30 percent unconsciously waiting for recognition for what we have done.

In performing our work, we act like good students. We have learned to wait for our teachers to grade us, compliment us, notice us, and—we hope—promote us. Just so, we wait and hope for our colleagues to tell us how good our report was, instead of criticizing us for the mistakes they found; for our bosses to appreciate aloud our last negotiation, instead of asking if that was all we could get; for higher management to use their X-ray vision to see us at our best and give us both psychic and financial

3

rewards instead of ignoring us. When waiting doesn't work—and it surely doesn't—we become resentful.

Our resentment grows. First we lament that we are not further along, that we weren't selected, that others who have done less or have been on the job for a shorter time were promoted over us. We complain to our families and friends while suppressing our disappointment at work. Then, after repeated slights, we begin indirectly to show our hostility at work. It grows worse each time we are overlooked. Sometimes we dream that we might be someone else, doing something else much more exciting. So we spend time looking up the details of other jobs, or researching various training programs. We exhibit the grass-is-greener syndrome, but we do less and less that is positive and active. We fall into a deadly trap in wanting only to do more work better. We get caught and stay stuck in the same job for years. We get caught watching others move up, feeling a mixture of envy and contempt. We get caught without having any way to draw attention to our achievements. We eat lunch alone. We avoid our co-workers—our peers, employers, and employees. In short, we pay with our lives.

This unspoken resentment narrows our vision and then limits our contributions. It hurts us and then we hurt everyone else with whom we come in contact. After a while, we act as a magnet, attracting others who are also looking for a sympathetic group, albeit a negative one. This group acts to confirm that we have been right all along; we are all victims caught in a terrible system. Together we remain righteously entrenched. By this time, the quality of our work has gone down as we spend more time waiting for approval. When it doesn't come, our grievances grow—from complaints about our supervisors and managers to complaints about our departments, our firms, our entire profession, and finally, written large, our whole society. But in the end, we have gone from a sustaining position to one of being resigned. We aren't willing to take responsibility for our failures or our successes.

## The Achievers

The *Achievers,* on the other hand, work not only harder and longer, but better and differently than the Sustainers. Unconsciously or not, they divide their work world totally differently than the Sustainers do. Certainly Achievers work longer hours. *New York* magazine has published several surveys on work weeks which reveal that well-known politicians, lawyers, doctors, publishers, and telecasters typically work from sixty to a hundred hours a week. These answers coincide with the responses successful people gave me. So when I talk about the 50 percent of their time that Achievers spend on doing their jobs well, that 50 percent represents a lot more time than the Sustainers' 70 percent. But hours spent working is hardly the only factor for success, and it is not the most crucial one. Success lies primarily in what we do with the other 50 percent of our work lives. That "other" separates the Achievers from the Sustainers, who don't get ahead simply because they do not or will not recognize the significance of those other nontechnical skills.

To achieve—that is, to make important contributions despite obstacles—it is important that we get recognition for what we have done or are about to do. Actively seeking versus passively waiting for recognition are poles apart and represent two different world views. Achievers have learned along the way to tell other people about the jobs or projects that they've done, what they've learned, and what they think are the next applications or steps. They know they must interact with others within their own departments, other departments, and the whole organization. Of course, talking about your good work or ideas is hardly new. Gilbert (of Gilbert and Sullivan) even wrote about it: "Blow your own trumpet, or trust me you haven't a chance." Good work counts to your advantage only if it is seen, heard, and somehow recognized. For how can we judge it if we haven't seen it? But the reverse is also true: if you don't want to be judged, don't display your work.

Those of us who are Achievers also enhance our careers by building contacts and alliances with others. We look for opportunities to establish new relationships and maintain our existing ones. There are many different reasons for creating and maintaining connections to others and their organizations. Connecting gives us perspective about how we work, provides us with different approaches to problems and sharpens our ideas of what is important, relevant, or new, and makes us visible to others like us.

Contacts also release us from a feeling of dependence, allowing us to be bolder in our thinking because we are no longer afraid that ours is the only job in the entire system. Sharing work ideas and experiences can be a source of support, a way to expand our understanding of the nature and potential of our jobs. And the more we know, the more our organization values and depends on us, allowing us more opportunity and freedom. All told, connecting with others is enriching and life-giving, and assures us of endless possibility and opportunity.

To be sure, we all slide back and forth between the two categories. But for too many minutes of every working hour, we live more as Sustainers. Why? What stops us Sustainers from becoming Achievers? The answer is painful. We Sustainers believe that performing the skills in that top 50 percent of extra activity beyond doing the job is *cheating*. We want success to come only from working hard, and doing our jobs well; we imagine that the breaks will come along the way.

The Sustainers among us are schizophrenic about success, because we want it and yet feel contempt for it at the same time. Because successful moves or strategies are hardly ever revealed in full, we project our beliefs onto them. Partly jealous and partly self-righteously enraged, we claim that Achievers knew the right people, pulled tricks, b.s.'d, and brown-nosed their way up, proving that most disgusting old adage, "Flattery will get you anywhere." We believe that making it is the direct result of either trickery or chance, and not deserved. At our worst, we imagine we are morally superior because success isn't happening to us.

These explanations of our own and others' success correspond to three of our folk sayings, which have been passed along to interpret or generalize about experience in the working world:

1. Success breeds success.
2. You have to be in the right place at the right time.
3. It's who you know, not what you know.

Although these expressions are meant to be cynical, they contain a hidden curriculum for success. Let me show you how.

## 1. Self-Presentation

*Success breeds success* points to the fact that people get jobs because of their good track records. Employers want proven winners, and generally consider a candidate's past and present work experience before they gamble on the future. The important thing here is how you interpret that experience for a potential employer. If you describe a project you worked on in terms of what you actually did, what you learned, whether it worked, what others thought/think about it, and how you would do it again, you control the way you present yourself and give the most positive interpretation of your past and present performance on the job.

In this kind of recounting, you are really being asked to sell yourself. While things go wrong in every project, at every turn, you need to demonstrate how you are capable, trustworthy, personable, yet relentless in getting the job done effectively and efficiently. But it only *sounds* simple. Unfortunately, we have been conditioned to represent ourselves as less than what we really are. Fears of being found out and seen as a fraud trigger inappropriate bragging or meekness. Our failures and weaknesses flood our memories and we kowtow out of the fear of taking new risks. Most of the time, it is we ourselves who give away the chance to demonstrate our abilities. It is infinitely easier to list what we'd like to improve or change about ourselves than to state what we're satisfied with, even proud of. And most of us state our deficiencies and call this negative-laden self-description *honest*. With such so-called honesty we underrepresent ourselves in too many situations. Without paying attention to what we are doing, we actually reinforce bad self-presentation. Almost no school, except the School of Hard Knocks, can break us of this habit and retrain us to give a truer and more positive picture of ourselves.

Here is an example of how vital self-presentation can be. I recently talked with a friend who is the director of training in one of the more prestigious psychoanalytic institutes in the country. He had just finished giving an oral examination to two psychiatrists in training at the institute. Psychiatrists spend at least seven years in medical school and psychiatric residencies, plus several years in their own personal therapy. Then, if they choose to be analysts, they spend an additional several years studying at an institute before they can be accepted as a full member. At the end of their training they must be tested again, in oral and written form, to be admitted to the institute. I was curious about the oral exam and asked my friend about the nature of the questioning and whether both candidates passed. He told me that only one question was asked to determine the fate of the two trainees. He added that only one passed. Then he told me the question: "What would you expect a one-year-old baby to do if its mother, upon bringing it to your office, had to leave the room for a few minutes?" I asked him to tell me the failing answer first: "I'd expect the baby to cry, being separated from its mother." The passing answer? "I'd expect the baby to cry, being separated from its mother. Now, separation anxiety is a complex issue, particularly at the age of only one. There are conflicting interpretations. According to those who hold with . . ."

Without prejudging, I asked my friend if he told the failing doctor why he failed. No. My guess was that the failing candidate would be in the library, trying to find out exactly what newly separated babies really do, or else he was raging against an unfair system. I asked my friend if he knew why the passing one passed. He laughed and said that fellow was always such a bullshitter. I asked if he regularly passed bullshitters and failed nonbullshitters. His tone of voice over the long-distance call carried the sound of disbelief at *my* crassness.

Now let's look at what happened. At first glance, it appears that the psychiatrists' answers are identical. The facts are there—both agree that the baby cries. But any serious interview or exam doesn't only measure one's knowledge of the facts. Often, there aren't any real facts, only interpretations, especially in psychiatry. The failing psychiatrist gave an answer and waited obediently; the passing one posted a probable answer and then revealed how it was that he came to know it. He provided some theory to let the examiner know that he was prepared, had read extensively, was reflective; he spoke as a colleague and was therefore likely to be a credit to the institute. He knew that the test was a vehicle for *Self-Presentation*. What the trainer wanted to ask but couldn't was, "Are you enough like us to warrant our letting you join our institute?" The first was not; he was still a student in the worst sense. But the second was; he knew, in addition to the facts, how to substantiate his answer with examples from psychiatric theory and practice.

All subjective tests are such vehicles for Self-Presentation, as are interviews. The questions are there to provoke a kind of dialogue, which gives you an opportunity to reveal who you are and what you know. It is a test, not of fact, but of Self-Presentation.

Here is another example, which is very different in situation but makes a similar point. A beautiful and talented young actress who had had a moderately active career on the Broadway stage came to Los Angeles to try to get work in the film industry. To support herself until she became established, she decided to do some commercials. But when her auditions with advertising agencies did not lead to any work, her agent told her that several auditioners had commented on her brooding and unfriendly behavior. He suggested that she try to change her attitude and present herself in a more positive way. Surprised at her lack of self-awareness, this young woman went over every one of her actions during the past several auditions and came up with the following changes. Instead of arriving at the agency wearing jeans and scarves, her face ready to be made up, she appeared in a simple shirt-dress, wearing her own makeup. Instead of using the reception room as the place where, hunched over in silent concentration, she projected herself into the role to be auditioned for, she rehearsed in her car and then stepped into the reception room as if it were her first stage, the receptionist now her first auditioner. She appeared to be a pleasant and attractive young woman instead of a sullen and frustrated actress in search of work. As a result, you can see her lovely face convincing you to buy soap, coffee, paper, and other household items.

There is no one true self to present, no limited "package" to learn. We must experiment with Self-Presentation and learn to select from *a wardrobe of behaviors,* just as we select from a wardrobe of clothes. We choose our dress according to the nature of a situation and our role therein. Just so, we want to be able to choose the behavior most effective and appropriate for us in each situation. Now it is easy to say that if we choose a role from a wardrobe of roles we are not being "ourselves." And not being oneself is considered being a phony, especially to the Sustainers. Yet we are different to our parents than we are to our children, different in our buying than in our selling, different to people we have invited into our homes than we are to strangers in restaurants. Psychological research indicates that the more diverse roles we have for different situations, the healthier we are. Learning to present yourself in the most appropriate and effective way is a major goal behind almost every modern psychotherapy—from Gestalt to Transactional Analysis, from Re-Evaluation Counseling to est. It is seen as a healthy state one toward which therapists guide their clients. But it is historically new. Only in this last century have we conceived of our world as being negotiated, a world in which we have the chance to shape our lives—our careers as well as our personal lives.

Now I know that negotiation is a loaded term, and I will talk about it in different ways throughout this book. For now, let me say that when you negotiate for more responsibility, a promotion, a bigger budget, or a new job, you must present yourself as someone who is worthy of whatever you are asking for. People see you according to the image you project. Often when you're starting out in your career you don't feel worthy or important, though you truly are, and you're afraid to ask for anything—or you think you deserve a raise, but you're afraid *they* don't think so. But you can learn to act as if you do deserve it (even if you don't think so or if you worry that your boss doesn't). The purpose of Self-Presentation is to act in our own best interest, and act as though we are the successful people that we want to be. That is the most valuable interpretation of the saying *success breeds success*.

## 2. Positioning

Successful people often attribute their success to *being in the right place at the right time*, a mere stroke of luck. But is it really luck to use a situation in a profitable way?

I think, instead, that strategic planning and purposeful striving are necessary prerequisites for making the most of every opportunity, and ultimately for making progress in your work.

As I questioned the Achievers in the course of my research, I found that not only had they been in the right place at the right time, but they also had been in many right places at the wrong time, in wrong places at the right time, and had even occasionally struck out altogether: wrong place, wrong time. I learned that successful people are in many places at many times, despite the sometimes indifferent reactions of others, and their own disappointments. They are always open to new situations, willing to see where they might lead. Such repeated experience cultivates their sense of opportunity, of where and when and, even more important, of how to act in different situations, and, of course, makes it all the more likely that something interesting or instructive will happen. For Achievers, trial-and-error positioning is a continuing process, a lifelong involvement rather than a way to get the lucky break.

Achievers never say that they have failed. Instead, when they try positioning themselves and they don't achieve what they had hoped to, they say "It didn't work out." Their choice of words reflects a positive attitude toward risk-taking. They know when to move on when things are not working out and learn not to blame themselves unrealistically for what Sustainers call failure.

A UCLA economist, Dr. Marilyn Kourilsky, has found similar differences among the behaviors of second-graders in her "mini-economy societies." Time after time she finds that successful students try several approaches to a given problem and, if none of them work, they move on to tackle the next problem. The average student, in contrast, tries the same approach repeatedly, until defeated by the self-imposed label of "failure." Just like those second-graders, some of us learn to be Achievers while the majority fall into the Sustainer category. We apply immediate self-blame: "I failed. I had better not try too much again or I might risk another failure."

Successful *Positioning* has nothing to do with one stroke of luck. Only the Sustainers among us wish that fate would be on our side and would reward us with the realization of our fondest dreams when we take our first bold steps. It is only through repeated efforts in experimentation and risk-taking that we achieve the confidence and awareness that enables us to approach people in an appropriate way, ask for what we want (whether it be advice, information, a raise, or a recommendation). Our repeated efforts to present ourselves in a positive way in situations that can be valuable to us are what ultimately put success in our way, and make it possible for us to realize our goals.

Positioning, then, is a step-by-step process of moving into an arena. Questions emerge: A temporary or a permanent arena? What should come next? Do you choose the situation at hand or one you really want, wherever it is? How do you make your move if you don't know what you really want? The process of careering which I propose provides a way of finding out—*picking* something *without precluding* everything else. I believe that Achievers, even when they are not sure of where they want to go, start by doing the best they can with the job at hand. They get involved in a variety of projects with different people, knowing that one thing will lead to another. Being active in and responsive to situations becomes a highly developed skill, though one that is often invisible to others. It requires an acute sensitivity, a keen awareness of what is going on—in the office, at a party, in any number of settings—and an instinct for turning problems into opportunities. And remember that you can develop this sensitivity through repeated experience, though you must be willing to be alert and receptive all the time.

Let me give you two examples of Positioning.

I was hired by a research corporation to hold a careering seminar for their research assistants, to motivate them to move up into project directors' positions, which would benefit both the corporation and themselves. These assistants were all highly qualified people, many with several advanced degrees, all with substantial experience and with the ability to give the attention to detail required of researchers. Here's how the system worked. Once research projects were finished, new ones had to be found. In the meantime, project managers and clerical staffs had to be kept on, and the researchers were not involved in billable project work. The researchers, then, had to be more than data collectors and report writers; for their own survival, they had to be able to generate new projects. They needed to be both hustlers and inventors. But their training kept them from thinking that either hustling or inventing is "clean." So, instead, most researchers looked to their various project managers for their next assignments.

My job, then, was to help the researchers find opportunities to Position themselves so that they could find (and recognize) potential projects and take advantage of emerging situations. They also needed to improve their Self-Presentations, using past successes to capture new interest. I asked the group to play researchers to their own projects to dicover ways to Position themselves and suggested that they (1) search for those projects that could be written up as in-house papers for circulation within their organization; (2) discover which findings from a finished project could well relate to or enhance present or future projects; and (3) generate a list of potential proposals building on what was significant in the past. I also urged them to go beyond their role of obedient student (Sustainer) and talk with their project leaders about more than just their research assignment. We rehearsed conversations about weekend activities, families, schooling, ambitions, even dreams and, of course, new project ideas. I encouraged them to use hallways not merely as routes from one place to another but as meeting places to exchange ideas and information about new proposals and projects. Over the succeeding two months the researchers went from a passive stance to an active one, from being dependent to being initiators, from diligent workers in office and library to active citizens of the corporation.

After the seminar the researchers reported back to me on their new successes. One researcher told me how he used a burglary as an opportunity to Position himself. His car had been stolen from the parking lot, along with several others. Appointed to a small task force to look for solutions, he found a simple, inexpensive way to reduce car theft and pilfering in the lot in suggesting that some nonfunctional structures that blocked the view of the security guards be removed. He had acted quickly, presenting himself as a person capable of tackling problems. He also offered a solution that would benefit others as well as himself. This might not seem like a great accomplishment, yet his actions caught the eye of important people who saw him taking initiative and solving a problem. He had demonstrated Positioning by taking an existing situation and acting on it in a constructive way, rather than letting the situation overwhelm him and hoping that someone else would set it right.

In the second case, the editor of an in-house newsletter had been fired when the computer system manufacturer he had worked for underwent a major reorganization. As he told me all that he had done for them, I realized that he had been doing more than what his job of editing called for. To see the scope of his ability, I had him bring in samples of his work, which included marketing surveys and advertising concepts. His work was indeed impressive but he was underselling himself. I had him call the department heads of a dozen computer firms in the city, all of whom he knew from professional associations, and talk briefly about some of his recent projects and surveys, and the application of his findings to the field. I also suggested that he offer an insider's view of his company's reorganization, of which his colleagues would be aware. As a result of the second call, he was hired to build a new research department, a job which far exceeded his former position in its responsibilities and rewards.

Some say his new position was only luck. It's true to a point; he was in the right place at the right time. But what served him above all were his contacts in the field. As a member of an association for computer professionals he was known for his imaginative contributions and for his reliability; he had built a reputation there, in a less competitive and more visible arena. It was important, of course, for him to let it be known that he was immediately available, but like anyone who has been fired, he felt depressed and uncertain of his talents. He needed to face the situation and act in a way that would be to his advantage. We rehearsed what he would say. He was not to complain and not to ask directly for help. He was to present himself as a competent professional who had something to offer to his colleagues. It worked. He turned loss into a considerable gain.

You can learn to jockey for Position and become highly skilled at it in the same way that you have become skilled at a sport or other activity. And just as you practice tennis to become a good player, you must practice Positioning to develop a sense of good times and right places to act. You have to experiment and take risks, try a new approach when an old one doesn't work. These are the ways in which you become skilled at anything, whether it be tennis, or skiing, or gourmet cooking. If you're willing to act, you'll be able to build your career-enhancing skills too.

## 3. Connecting

Success is often explained in terms of *who you know, not what you know*. This rule of advancement is most often attributed with contempt to "movers" who seem to have "made it" by knowing people in high places, rather than through any particular talent of their own. We are trapped by our belief that those people cheat the system in using their connections, that they are frauds who take on jobs they know little about. The consequence of this thinking is that we are afraid to make those vital connections, and that we distrust our capacity to grow into a new position. We must turn this thinking around and realize that knowing other people in our field is crucial to our success, and that as long as we have something to learn, we can continue to grow. If we feel that we must be *totally* prepared *before* we enter experience, we will be forever trapped by the dangerous model of the good student.

*Connecting*, like Self-Presentation and Positioning, involves experimenting and risk-taking. With practice we can become skilled at promoting ourselves through contact with others. Connecting is another way of actively approaching experience.

An example from my own life will help me to make my point. At an advertising party a young couple came up and told me that they were intrigued by my organization's name on my name tag. I told them that I was very pleased that they had spoken to me. The young man said that it was his wife's idea, and that she always spoke to strangers, which often embarrassed him. I then asked him what it would take to make that night a memorable one for him. Meeting someone who would bring him new business? Meeting someone whose freshness of thought would excite his own imagination? In other words, what were his goals for the evening? He said that he often wanted to meet people, but found it hard to approach them. I agreed that cocktail parties where everyone is a stranger are always hard; they still are for me. But if Connecting is a goal, you have to start somewhere. How to do it without embarrassment is the tricky part. So I suggested that he consider a different scenario for the evening—that is, that he consider himself the party's host instead of its guest.

I asked him what he would do if he were the host. Introduce himself to people he didn't know and then introduce them to each other? Make sure people knew where food and drinks were? Watch out for lulls in conversations or bring over new people to an already formed small group? He laughed at the difference between the active role of the host and the passive one of the guest. A host is expected to do things for others, while a guest is allowed to sit back and receive attention. There was nothing to stop this man from playing the role of host even though he wasn't the actual host; there is nothing to stop any one of us from being far more active in many situations than we have been heretofore.

Expanding the hosting idea to the world at large can change your life perspective. Start small, while standing in line at a supermarket or a bank or a theater, where you can experiment with making contact with the people surrounding you. We all crave interaction; yet that pernicious old rule that we shouldn't talk to strangers until we are introduced narrows our chances for making interesting contacts.

One time on a train from Philadelphia to New York I sat next to a man who was a dishwasher at Madison Square Garden and learned how Madison Square Garden works, how he felt about his job, and what kinds of other experiences he had had. He excitedly told me his philosophy of life, and shared some of his plans for the future. After we got off the train, he walked me to the corner for a cab, checked out and discharged the first one, settled on the second, tipped the driver for me and told him how to get me to where I was going. To my delight, he had become host to New York City for me.

Such a relationship counts whether it is long-lasting or fleeting. What was important for me is that I took the opportunity to create a connection. Yet most of us pass up these chances because we are too afraid of each other. And while it is good sense to be careful, it is also foolish and wasteful to fear everyone. If you look around you'll discover endless opportunities to connect with others. Our career survival depends on our development of this skill.

When we stop to think of it, knowing other people is as vital to our advancement in work as it is to our personal development. We may be as reluctant to approach people in our field as we are to talk to a stranger on a plane. We imagine that we are mere flatterers, trying to get something for nothing, or that we are imposing ourselves on another's privacy. Here again we have to change our thinking, and realize that going to others for help or encouragement is as much a part of making progress as is presenting ourselves in a positive way. After all, we are willing to help our friends find jobs, and to think of ways to promote our staff people when they're ready to move on.

The buddy system, based on Connections, allows us to pursue and be pursued by others in our profession without fear or embarrassment. The fact is that we *are* dependent on each other. It's just that simple, and too often we refuse to acknowledge it. We get stuck in thinking that what matters is only how good our work is and how hard we work at being good. I don't mean to imply that hard work is not a requisite; I repeat, it is, *but* there is more that we have to do to get ahead. Consider the examples of these two men, both excellent in their work, who lacked Connections and wondered why they were not getting more from what they did.

A forty-year-old dentist came to me for consultation on the redirection of his career. He had recently joined the dental department of a major university, as a visiting lecturer without tenure. He had had a long, personally unsatisfying history in the military and had made intermittent stabs to establish a private practice. He had all the obvious attributes for success; he was tall, handsome, personable, smart, capable, dilligent, even artistic. Yet his career wasn't working. Why? He had no Connection with anyone—not even with dentists in professional associations who were in private practice, let alone on the faculty. He was a loner. In his leisure time he camped alone and painted landscapes. His immediate family was his only social network.

Our first plan was for him to practice Connecting, by lunching with his director, requesting committee positions in his director's professional society as well as within the university, and by getting acquainted with those dentists whose work he admired. He also had to take a look at his own research, organize it into suitable journal articles, and then submit them to various journals of dentistry.

Of course, such Connecting worked. He was eventually noticed by directors and administrators, asked about his new work, and invited to serve on several committees. It didn't come easily, however. At first, he was reluctant to get involved with others and uncomfortable about what he pejoratively called "chitchat"—the small talk that can, with time, serve as a bridge to the discussion of ideas and to a more personal exchange. In time, as his efforts were rewarded, he loosened up and took pleasure from his newfound skill.

Another client, about thirty years old, an executive in a multi-national food organization, was considering a move to a related industry. But, like the dentist, he was a loner, disliked socializing in business circles, and consequently had few professional contacts. He also felt he would be taking advantage of people to use them as connections in his search for a new position. As we talked I realized that he was hiding behind his idea of "using" people, and that in fact he was afraid to approach them. He hadn't had much practice talking to people in a personal way. Reluctantly he agreed to make an effort to meet new people and to look at any encounters with a positive attitude. But he wanted to wait until he returned from a business trip to Japan. I told him that he had a perfect place to start—on the plane.

His first assignment was to talk to other passengers and exchange broad-scale business information.

He had good beginner's luck and happened to sit next to a businessman who has since become an invaluable contact for him. What wasn't luck, however, was that he spoke to this man; rather than withdrawing, he made himself open to the possibility of an exchange. The initial effort was exciting and the result satisfying. Now my client would have to take the next step and get to know his business associates in a social context, to mix business with pleasure, something he had never done. Fortunately he followed the advice he paid for, and eventually, with hard work and determination, he was able to make the most of the opportunities that came his way. He found himself with many new business contacts and personal friendships. He gradually came to the realization that using contacts is a respectable behavior, not a way to take advantage of or cheat others.

Connecting expands possibilities—in work and in life —for ourselves as well as for others. Connecting encourages us to share our experiences and ideas, it reinforces our experimenting, and provides us with new approaches to our work and our lives in general.

Self-Presentation, Positioning and Connecting are essential prerequisites for successful careering, and I have found through my research that Achievers unconsciously fulfill these requirements in every aspect of their lives, both professional and social. But many of us who have trouble getting ahead are held back by our belief system, which is made up of fears and lies. Let's take a closer look at that system and try to rid ourselves of many misconceptions.

# CHAPTER TWO

# False Assumptions

*The cat, having sat upon a hot stove lid, will not sit upon a hot stove lid again. Nor upon a cold stove lid.*

—MARK TWAIN

## Merit Is Its Own Reward

At the core of the Sustainers' actions is the belief that if we do our jobs well enough, we will be recognized, encouraged, given more opportunity, transferred, promoted. We think that if we study hard enough, perfect our craft well enough, then we'll have Truth on our side. We will become the authority that others will notice and appreciate. Wrong!

Our dependence on the rewards of merit comes about through careful teaching. We aren't born knowing it. In fact, it's just the opposite. We are born to be risk-takers and explorers. Yet our own institutions—our schools, families, religions—teach us to act against ourselves, to act against our best interests.

I see the results of our wrong concepts everywhere I go. At brunch the other day, I talked with a sculptor, a good one, one whose work should be tremendously popular. What was he doing? He was sitting and waiting for his New York gallery agent to arrange something. What was the gallery agent doing? Holding, if not hiding his work, was my guess. Why was he just sitting waiting in California for something to happen? Why wasn't he busy making contact with art editors, collectors, possible patrons, other artists, art leagues? Because he believed he would be taken care of, he was spending his time perfecting his work.

In Westwood, while standing in line for a Saturday night movie, I met a young poet who told me he had had some success and acclaim while still in his teens, but for several years his career had been in a decline. I asked him what he was doing to continue making his poetry known—where he was reading it, submitting it, talking about it. I thought of local radio and television talk shows as one way. After all, his poetry, as he told me, was about popular ideas. And poetry is an ideal form for talk shows—short, interpretive, dramatic, emotional. I can still hear his response: "Going after such publicity is degrading to me as an artist." Where do we learn to perceive these separate categories of work or art versus the business of promoting what we do? On the Dick Cavett show, Bruce Dern, the gifted actor, revealed that he lost the first half of his acting career by not recognizing that in addition to being an art, acting was also a business that had to be treated accordingly.

I have interviewed many successful people in all kinds of careers about the skills that were vital to their work. Comedians, lawyers, economists, financial writers, stockbrokers—all were very bitter about what schooling had left out. Some said that they had had to unlearn what they learned in school—that there are such things as right answers, that the one with the highest score is rewarded, that passive, obedient behavior means cooperation, that to ask for or receive help is cheating. All these attitudes, which we learned early in our lives, work against us in the working world and in social contexts as well. Our schooling did not provide us with the skills we need to be successful.

Let me give you a specific example. Joan Levine is president of Hall & Levine Advertising Agency and winner of the 1977 Advertising Leader of the Year award. She told me that the most crucial thing she learned at the beginning of her career was to give up her old ideas of what was considered good work. She learned instead to persevere, writing variations of copy until a client accepted her work. At the same time, she had to learn how to maintain her confidence, and to not consider it a crushing defeat when a client rejected all or even part of her copy. She said that she was not trained to do this and in school had always received a single grade for a one-time effort. But advertising is a lot different from schooling. In writing copy for advertising, you essentially have one job that you must do over and over until the client accepts it. You earn your *A* only then, whether or not you thought it your best effort. What Joan Levine learned was something more than tenacity, something beyond having the "right answers." What she learned was the business of work. Just because an ad is good does not necessarily mean it's accepted. And she learned that she could indeed offer several versions without compromising her artistic talent.

Achievers hold a view of life that is different from that held by Sustainers. Achievers believe in a negotiated world whereas Sustainers believe in a "fair" system (although those Sustainers who have been hurt the most become cynical). This essential difference dictates concomitant attitudes and actions. Achievers act as willing participants in the whole work process, negotiating their way along. They make new rules as well as play according to existing ones. Wanting to both give and get more, they are often labeled aggressive by those too timid to try.

## Authority Is the Best Teacher

A man called me urgently, late one night, desperate to change his job.

HIM:    I hate my job as a troubleshooter for a local truck rental firm. I'm ready for a career change. I want you to do vocational testing for me.

ME:     I don't give such tests. I've found that they tell only where you've been, who you've been, and what you've been exposed to. They don't tell you where you should go.

HIM:    I don't care about that; I want another vocational test. The one I took before told me that I should be a musician.

ME:     Are you musical? Does that fit you?

HIM:    No.

ME: Do you play any instrument or compose, or sing, or even listen to music?

HIM: No. Just tell me what I should do.

ME: What are the things about your current job you like?

HIM: Nothing at all.

ME: Are you willing to explore one or two avenues of opportunity there as well as think about a change?

HIM: Not really. I just want you to tell me what to do, considering my test results and my trouble-shooting job.

ME: There is nothing I can suggest except a glib "Whistle while you work!"

I relate this incident because it represents the core of what we believe about career choice. Although not too many of us sound like that troubleshooter, we nonetheless act like him in several ways. First, he believed that if I were a real testing authority I would know what he should do. He depended on teachers and tests, like fortune-tellers, for this vital information about his own life choices. He believes, like so many of us, that there is one right thing to do or be and that someone else knows what that is. It is as if each of us had a perfected version of ourselves inside of us, with obviously developed talents waiting to be recognized by an expert. The troubleshooter was hoping that I'd be that expert, test him, and pronounce something like, "Aha, you should be a dentist. Throw off your trucking uniform and enroll immediately in dental school."

Most of us have had some kind of testing, believing it would act as our divining rod. Even though the trucker knew that such test results had provided unreliable information before, he still wanted to believe in them. He hoped for another, better test. He wanted someone else to tell him what to do. But though I can't argue that vocational tests have no value—certainly they have some —they do not do what we want them to do. They are not good indicators for the present or the future. They are based on a limited range of jobs which doesn't take into account the fact that one-third of all our known jobs are newly created every decade. And they don't take into consideration the fact that for the most part our work grows out of current situations.

My own vocational test scores revealed that my aptitude lay in chemistry. But since I was a girl student, I was told I'd better learn shorthand so I could be a secretary in a chemical firm. And frankly, I didn't want to be a chemist or a biologist. The fact is that the tests had nothing to do with my real enthusiasms, nor do I think they accurately measured my capacity to perform in different fields. But nonetheless we are attracted to authority, and I believe that we're trained from the beginning to look to others for answers to questions that we can only find in ourselves. Consider what happens when we first go to school, as innocents, hoping to be shaped and prepared for some life career. What happens is not only that we are being shortchanged, but that we are being hurt. And the scars and deformities remain even twenty or fifty years after we have left school. Let me tell you how.

School relies on right answers instead of appropriate answers. Stop and think about that word: *appropriate*. The notion of there being one right answer hurts us in several ways. First, those of us who didn't (or wouldn't) make the grade often felt branded and have gone through life expecting a *C* or an *F* in everything we do. Some of us who didn't get to college feel that we are the only ones who don't know the right answer; everyone who went to college learned it. Second, others of us who did well and were rewarded with grades or scholarships often still live out our lives feeling as if we are frauds. Although we knew how to give the teacher what he or she wanted, we don't necessarily feel knowledgeable. The result is that too many of us still wait in terrific fear of being "found out"—in the next task by the next supervisor, client, agent, committee, or judge. As students in a merit system, we have been "promoted" from one grade to another almost automatically without knowing anything about how to improve our own presentation of ourselves. We hardly ever understand the politics of topic selection for papers and projects, or the politics of interpersonal skills, not only with teachers but with other students.

We learned many of the wrong things early in our lives and, as a result, are not adequately prepared for many of the things life demands of us. In fact, the skills and behaviors we learn are opposite to those we need to be successful, such as teamwork, follow-through, the tenacity to right what is wrong, the ability to determine appropriate solutions given certain constraints, and many other attitudes and approaches to people and problems that are essential in our working lives and that help us define who we are.

## Getting There by Careful Mapping

The third lie is that planning ahead for a career is the way to success. From the time we enter elementary school we are asked: "What do you want to be when you grow up?" We're asked to think seriously about a profession in high school, select a major in college, and choose a specialty in graduate school or a particular training program in business. Interviewers in personnel departments ask us where we'd like to be in five years. And life-planning services ask us to project our lives and to begin to label steps and strategies for the future.

All this is based on the so-called scientific notion of being able to define the world and to know what is to come. It ignores new situations, changing circumstances, and unexpected opportunities. The mapping theory ignores experience as a real teacher in shaping what we like and don't like, or the emergence of an interest in a related or different field. And it assumes that we can make choices based solely on our family's interests and ambitions, the often narrow attitudes of our school counselors, fantasies about work that we've drawn from movies and television, or our limited work and life experience. Intelligent choosing based on these ideas is next to impossible, yet we all feel we must choose, and so we do, without quite knowing why. Thus we don't learn how to choose or, even worse, we don't learn to want something for ourselves. We think we are picking what we want to be—doctor, lawyer, teacher—when we are doing what society tells us we ought to do, given our families and our educational opportunities. We have become, after all, a nation of consumers rather then creators—we consume others' dreams rather than realize our own.

## Manipulation Is Always Bad and Must be Avoided

Fear of manipulation immobilizes us. Yet the word *manipulate* means to take things in hand, to take charge of a situation. It's true that manipulation can hurt or help, depending on the motivations and intentions of the manipulator. But I am talking about a positive, not a negative, manipulation of behavior. Positive manipulation has the power to motivate others, and essentially reinforces good work and encourages people to be more productive or even innovative. When we are positively manipulated, we are pushed to learn more, to think better, to contribute more significantly—in short, to grow. Recent research on the psychology of learning indicates that learning reinforced with positive encouragement is a lot more significant than learning without such reinforcement. When we are given the opportunity to highlight or showcase our accomplishments to others in our organization or profession, we feel encouraged about our past efforts and our future ones. Our recognized achievement also spurs others to tell us their own successes, and sometimes also encourages them to compete, in the healthiest sense, for attention.

Yet often we see business and professional people who manipulate the system in a negative way to pay them not for their contribution, but for their loyalty. I was recently asked by officers of a large company to weed out their deadwood—those persons who had been working in the same job for at least twelve years without receiving any promotion and without contributing anything beyond their time to the company. Those people, maintained the officers, were there only for their paychecks. Like parasites, they didn't think of their work as their responsibility. They performed their tasks perfunctorily, doing only what was assigned to them, and had become a part of that gray class known as nine-to-fivers. What the company wanted instead—and was willing to pay for—were employees who felt a responsibility to improve both the product and the process. Although most of us wouldn't classify ourselves as deadwood, nonetheless some of us have been in the same jobs for too long. Too many of us have resigned ourselves to these jobs and really work only for the salary and fringe benefits. Too many of us are cheating ourselves as well as our organizations of our creativity, our ingenuity, our ability to take command of a task, and to give direction and meaning to our work.

Let me share an experience of a different nature on this same topic of manipulation. A professor of psychology from a leading university wrote me a letter of apology for her hostile behavior during my seminar on successful careering. She had questioned every part of my theory and had refused to participate in any exercise. But, afterward, reflecting on her intense reaction, she discovered that she felt rage at her own division between what she preached and what she actually practiced in her work. Although she taught a theory of communication, she never incorporated her ideas into her everyday interaction with her own students, or people in other departments. She found that she considered success to be measured only scholastically. She had been acting in the Sustainers' matrix, doing her job really well and strictly avoiding anything that smacked of manipulation. Her apology also indicated to me that she would strive for a clearer, more direct, honest communication of who she is and would reconsider what positive trade-offs she wants from other people. She exemplifies what I have found: the kinds of success I am talking about are generally based on a *quid pro quo,* "something for something."

To be used well is what we all crave. Being used well means others value who we are by considering us as resources; they seek our advice, opinions, connections. It confirms our experience and affirms our importance. We all need to be needed, to use and be used in rewarding ways. To refuse to manipulate is to refuse to initiate action and, in being passive, we give up a most valuable part of our human nature. We relinquish our power to others, inviting them to do with us as they will. And worse, we struggle to find the best ways to serve instead of negotiating for what we want.

## Happiness Is Money, Power, and Status

I have found in the lives of the Achievers whose work lore I have collected that happiness is the by-product of contribution and its reciprocal element, recognition. As humans we crave action, as well as reaction to what we do. We have a need to be seen. And, like the land we live on, we produce or lie fallow. Consider the waste of those of us who find no meaning in work, who are barred from work for whatever reason, or who are suddenly stripped of that meaning in retirement. We need to work and most of us make work, whether or not we have to for economic reasons. But how to work successfully is the best-kept secret of this age.

Success in careering has in large part been culturally defined as money, power, and status. There's nothing inherently wrong with this definition, but it doesn't go far enough. Successful careering also has personal meaning—job satisfaction, peace of mind, challenge, involvement. Its highest meaning may lie in contributing to the world, not just taking from it. According to the *Oxford English Dictionary*, the first meaning of *success* is movement of one step after another. *Career,* according to the same dictionary, means progress through life. When you think about it, forward movement and progress mean the same. In the most profound sense, the processes of careering and succeeding must be synonymous.

# ☐ PART II

□ **CHAPTER THREE**

# Critical Career Competences

From my own experience and that of many others, I have learned that insight isn't worth anything unless it leads to action. In our culture, what we do is who we are.

The skills that I call *Critical Career Competences* are ones that enable us to pursue opportunities for ourselves as well as enhance opportunities for others. They make it possible for us to be more active—to *do* more—in our jobs, to enlarge our area of responsibility, to take more risks in our careers, and as a result to expand our knowledge and expectations of ourselves and of others. This is a new definition for success.

In studying the lives of successful lawyers I found that within the three areas that I have defined—Self-Presentation, Positioning, and Connecting—there exist these hidden but critical skills or competences. I originally identified the Critical Career Competences as a result of in-depth interviews on the career lives of successful lawyers for my doctoral dissertation entitled *Careering: Identifying Critical Career Competences from Everyday Lawyering.* From my experience with other professions and disciplines I knew that the skills I was searching for had to be generic, applying to everyone, no matter what the field or the level of attainment. That I interviewed lawyers was more an arbitrary choice than a conscious decision to adhere to any predetermined set of criteria in choosing subjects. At first I had no criteria for defining success. Our cultural definition is money, power, and status and, I would add, contribution and progress. Each of us would probably add something else—perhaps satis-

31

faction, challenge, or peace of mind. But regardless of the definition of success, I was eager to find out how people moved ahead in their careers and to share these findings both in a theoretical framework and in a practical guide. A theory and practice of careering must grow out of what actually happens in successful people's lives. This is, then, the lore of careering—a collection of the vital but largely undefined interpersonal, nontechnical skills that comprises positive strategies for promoting ourselves, our colleagues, our organizations, and our professions in mutually beneficial ways.

These six Critical Career Competences cut across all disciplines and levels. I have used them to coach all kinds of clients—lawyers, doctors, psychologists, executives, foremen, secretaries, entrepreneurs, teachers. I have helped people to build their reputations, to negotiate for more responsibility as well as money, and to take up new challenges in general. And some have moved up, or over, or out from where they were, while others have revved up what they already had going, and still others have, at whatever age, started something completely new.

*To Experience Doing* means building a wardrobe of behaviors from a number of diverse activities and projects, career-related or not. Only in this way can you extend the boundaries of your self-imposed and limited circle of possibility and ability. In a very real and contemporary sense, your actions and your work—not your intentions—now define you. That you have limited or do limit yourself by not having more experience in doing— in sports, in clubs, in competitions and cooperatives— keeps you bound in by fear in a self-made paralysis.

*To Risk Linking* is the skill of combining risk-taking and connecting to people, to organizations, and to ideas. This skill builds on the human use of human beings, on starting associations and sharing networks and resources. It leaves behind the old childhood model of not joining until you're invited, of not speaking until you're spoken to.

*To Show Belonging* is the skill of enhancing your own organization by paying attention to it, caring for it, supporting it, creating a more productive and interactive department or division. It goes beyond coming in on time, doing your work, and collecting your salary.

*To Exhibit Specializing* is the skill of demonstrating your worth to your organization, apart from just doing your job well. It includes figuring out not only what you're particularly good at in your job but also what others who work with you need you for, apart from your specific work-related responsibilities. Some of these special roles might be the problem solver, the academic, the organizer, the listener, or the comedian. There is an important interplay between these talents and the actual work that you are assigned to do, and you can get recognition for both.

*To Use Catapulting* is the skill of using your business associates or job-related contacts and sometimes your friends to connect you to others who can be of help to you in your career. These people who provide the access you would never have by yourself are sometimes called resources, or experts, or sponsors, or mentors. Implicit contracts between you and your resources exist which require your show of appreciation, a report on your progress, and loyalty in return for connections and ideas.

*To Magnify Accomplishing* is the supreme skill, the culmination and synthesis of all the foregoing ones. It is the displaying of your work and ideas before many publics. It involves active participation in your organization, taking on leadership in professional associations, speaking and moderating panels before community and other business groups, and writing articles in trade journals. Magnifying Accomplishing is a natural result of successful careering and comes later in your career when you are an established member of a profession and can reach outside the boundaries of your particular job. As a person with expertise and years of experience, you are in a position to share what you know, to be a mentor to others, and to take part in the shaping of your profession.

As you learn these skills (or discover them within yourself) and make them a part of your professional life, you will find that they are all a part of a general attitude and mode of behavior, that one skill or competence doesn't work in a vacuum apart from all the others. You will see that they overlap and take strength from each other, though at times you will emphasize one skill over the others. It is important to look at them one at a time, to get a clear understanding of the different components of a career-enhancing behavior, and to see how they work as a unit to help you reach your immediate and long-range goals.

# ☐ CHAPTER FOUR

# Experiencing Doing

*Knowing is not enough; we must apply.*
*Willing is not enough; we must do.*
>                              —GOETHE

Experiences are not only what happens; they are what they mean to us, what they mean to others, how we remember them, and what they teach us about the world. With practice we develop a faculty—another nose, if you will—about how to shape with our intentions what is about to happen or what has just occurred. Experiences are not only life; they are lessons in living. But we all have to learn to "smell them." That's what Experiencing Doing is about. As a skill it is set apart from the others because it is more personal than career-related, though it can and does have a profound effect on how we move in our careers.

We enter the world with unlimited possibilities. Our human inheritance should destine each of us to be explorers, discoverers, creators, developers—in short, geniuses in every conceivable pursuit: art, science, relationships. But most of us don't experience our lives that way.

We all, in fact, have biographies complete with interesting stories and worthwhile accomplishments. We make choices, both large and small, of who to be and what to do. How, then, can we account for the disparity between what is possible, and what we settle for? Our explanation to ourselves is that we are tied down by circumstances.

The boundaries of our lives are first drawn by our families and our backgrounds. Their experiences, expectations, and beliefs determine what we expect and want. Add to these the cultural restraints of race, sex, class, even birth order, and we can see how narrow the arena is in which we act.

Because we are black or brown or yellow, we are taught to expect fewer opportunities than those open to whites. Because we are female, we are trained to be supporters, without the strength to lead, needing protection, and without ability in quantitative or scientific pursuits. Because we are male, we are taught to withhold personal expression and deny our emotions. Because we are middle children, we are taught to fight for the attention that may never come. Because we are Catholic or Jewish or Fundamentalist, we are caught in a difference that can lead to isolation, if not hostility, in a Protestant mainstream. Because we were out of work in the Depression, we have vowed to stay with our jobs forever and put away every penny for a future we won't live to see.

Because our teachers and our families may have cut off our early attempts at expression, we silently agree to be inhibited about singing, dancing, drawing, writing, answering aloud, and daring to think or develop our own views. We learn, then, only to give the company line, whether that "company" is an esoteric classics department in any Ivy League university or a political machine in a major city.

Such restrictions make it hard for us to choose appropriate situations for our individual contributions to life, and consequently we limit our possibilities by conforming to a negative past. Too often we mistakenly call what is left, after fear and hurt have taken their toll, our personality. Whatever we call it, that is all we have to operate from unless we do something to expand it or to reshape it. And we ourselves are our only reshapers.

This first skill, Experiencing Doing, is a testing and stretching over time of our boundaries of possibility, a continuing discovery of new aspects of ourselves. It is also the cultivation of an attitude toward life, one that propels us into experience rather than withdrawing us from it. At the outset, we cannot know the whole of life's design. That comes only from experimenting, our attempts to know who we are and who we may become. Such experimentation comes only from Experiencing Doing. Our sense of identity cannot come from others' concepts of us. And it is experimentation alone that gives us the ability to not be deceived by such destructive criticisms as "Don't you think you're too short (fat, Catholic, poor) to make it in politics?" "How can you assume any leadership in that organization until you conquer your stuttering (agonizing, fears, marital problems)?" "Better not try without any prior experience." "Give up graphics; you're only average."

Experiencing Doing, then, is more than just the separate acts of experiencing or doing. It is the combination of both; the first (Experiencing) helps us understand and derive meaning from the second (Doing). In the process of Experiencing Doing, many things happen that could never happen otherwise. We begin to delineate our likes and dislikes, make preferences, learn to observe with a critical eye, and gradually eliminate awkward pieces of ourselves. That is, through experience we form judgments about ourselves and about others. We act, experiment, practice, and create occasions for developing and exhibiting skills that had not otherwise been available to us. We take what we have to start with and we learn to make something of it, something more than we imagined to be possible at the beginning.

Here's a card-game metaphor. You have to play the hand that you're dealt. You play it the best way you can. Rather than waiting for a better hand in order to start again or, worse, throwing in the hand before the game is played, reflect on and play each hand fully. Learn its lessons. Appreciate the irony of a good hand that's beaten by a lucky stroke. Enjoy winning in an unexpected way. In this way you can build up a sense of confidence in your ability to *play* the game, whatever your hand, and whether you win or lose. Experiencing Doing is a process of becoming comfortable with your own actions, reactions, and opinions.

Experiencing Doing is something that almost all of us practice unknowingly early in our lives. It is made up of our involvement in diverse, even random, short-lived activities that may have an extraordinary influence on our attitudes. The more we experience anything, the more opportunities we have to test our different roles, abilities, fears, even dreams, and to define our evolving selves.

In mapping out the lives of the successful lawyers I learned that each one was full of varied and intense involvements that led to the next more rigorous ones. I must say, however, that these lawyers never recognized that their current success might have had its roots in past commitments to sports, music, and student government. When I first questioned them about their early lives, they answered by stating what they did as children. But when I continued to probe, their responses suggested that their early activities provided them with their first opportunities to develop the behaviors that they were to build on throughout their lives. Although they were Experiencing Doing initially for the pure joy of it, they were, looking back, defining and redefining themselves and building confidence through action and interaction.

For example, as children many of the lawyers whose lives I studied participated in school plays. I must admit that at first I tossed this information aside. But when so many remembered in detail the titles of the plays and the names of their parts, although they exhibited apparent amnesia about other aspects of elementary school, I began to take their playacting seriously. Consider what skills were necessary (an attitude can be a skill) and what experiences were gained in playing the prince or the neglected daughter in *Cinderella*. Their willingness to try out for a part means that they were willing to face the responsibility of acceptance or the pain of rejection—a risk that many of us in our adult lives refuse to take. They had to confront competitive feelings with regard to the assigning of leading and supporting roles. They also had to learn their parts and rehearse in front of the other players, which left them open to peer judgment. Taking direction, a highly underestimated skill, requires making positive moves in response to the criticism offered by a faculty sponsor or teacher. Skill is needed to deal with the sure-to-happen fear labeled stage fright. Receiving praise or criticism after the performance is an unthought-of risk that makes or breaks ego strength for the next trial. All in all, it is no mean task when little girls and boys Experience Doing in a school play.

To nobody's surprise, many of the lawyers interviewed were also on their schools' debate teams. Yet the actual tasks of preparing and performing the debate were secondary to the Experience of Doing. Student debaters learned to be supportive of their team, whether they were winning or losing, and whether they were the hosts or the guests of other clubs. Then, too, debating typically led these students to other, more visible speaking roles which, in turn, emphasized their ability to present themselves well in public.

In short, the act of participating in a school play or a debate is more analogous to life than being a good student can ever be. The same kinds of learning and skills, both social and technical, are as important in business and professional life as they are in drama clubs, debate teams, 4-H projects, scouting, or any other extracurricular activity.

Running for school office also required a range of behaviors that were to be crucial to the lawyers' successful careering. The pattern of action (Doing) that I discovered in my interviews began, as always, with a willingness to try. Running for a school office (or for governor) requires that you sell yourself to others. Selling yourself to others means presenting your strengths. To run for office, you must persuade others to support you, and when you have their support, you must give them active, visible campaign roles and encouragement when there are setbacks. You must decide to be consistently "on"— to act in the best light with the best answers, unflappable, prepared, unargumentative, personable, and constantly rational and reassuring. You must be willing to repeat the same speech, with slight variations, freshly and coherently and with absolute confidence—an invisible skill to others.

I found that in most cases it is more important to run for an office than to win. In my interviews with lawyers who ran for, but did not get elected to, student or local government positions, I was hesitant at first to discuss running and losing for fear of embarrassing them. But, to my surprise, the experience of running for office had in itself been a life-transforming act. Most of those who were defeated candidates for such positions as city council member or members of a school board spoke of "secondary" victories. Being publicly visible in their campaigns had brought them invitations from committees, businesses, political coalitions. Experiencing running for office had taught them the value of self-promotion and visibility and had enhanced their skills of leadership.

We all need opportunities and situations to Experience Doing. It is important for us to seek out what we might call a training ground for experimenting, for trying on new behaviors, expressing our opinions, and ultimately building a confidence in our ability to achieve in any arena.

A careful look at your own past will reveal more about your own early learning than you might guess. And, of course, Experiencing Doing is not limited to early life. It is still possible for you to have varied opportunities now, even if you were denied them early in your life. Such experiencing is developmental, continuous through life—not limitied to any one age. You will reduce fear of doing only by doing, by building a repertoire of experiences as a base of support for every new life adventure. They will give you new perspective and understanding of who you are and how you want to move.

I asked my lawyer-subjects to tell me some stories from their lives, and many of them were about army experiences. I was particularly struck by two of these stories, in which attitudes were radically different, and which show how an opportunity was either recognized or disregarded. One private was assigned as typist at the headquarters office for a military base. He used this opportunity to become acquainted with all of the top-ranking officers and to carefully read the reports that he typed. He also made it his business to talk to the officers on all kinds of topics. This resulted in their taking a personal interest in promoting him. The private was building an environment of success, whether he knew it or not.

On the other hand, another man who had a talent for understanding psychological and mathematical theory was assigned to do psychological testing of servicemen in World War II. Instead of seeing it as a possible opportunity to enhance his ability to deal with new and strange situations, he contemptuously chalked it up to one more activity he had to endure. He actually discovered in the performance of these psychological tests that as the administrator of the test he could predict, and therefore determine, the outcome of the test, depending on his interaction with the testee. What that meant, of course, was that the test was neither very valid nor very reliable. But instead of seizing his finding as an opportunity to report it or change it, he refused to get involved. He created a prison for himself and was relieved when his assignment was finally completed. He threw away an opportunity to Experience Doing. He made a bad memory of his experience.

The chances to Experience Doing come every day at every turn, always unexpectedly. They do not come in clearly labeled packages and often are missed. But chances, once taken, become memorable because we learn from the resulting experiences.

Experiencing Doing is so critical that without it we cannot progress in our careers and in our lives. In fact, those people with little experience outside a routine job are the only ones who do *not* do well with my career coaching. Their fear is so intense that they are unable to go after what they want the most. In 1973 I did some relevant research with a colleague and gave a life-planning workshop at UCLA Extension, documenting what happened to the 125 women who signed up for a two-day workshop, two weeks apart. Sixty of them were housewives and/or volunteer workers and as such were not paid for their work. Sixty-five were women who worked in such disparate jobs as file clerk, lawyer, pediatrician. At the end of the first day, the participants were given assignments, one of which was to interview people about their jobs.

Those women who were not paid for their work were also those who had very little other experience. They didn't do any part of the assignments, giving as excuses that they didn't have enough time, that they didn't know how to begin, or that they had had to deal with immediate family crises. On the other hand, those women who were paid for their work and who were richer in experience than the volunteers did all of the assignments. Some said they would have liked to have done more or to have done them better or differently. While one large workshop does not provide conclusive evidence, my own practice as a career coach proves again and again that inexperienced people need to have many more experiences of all kinds in order to move in *any* kind of career.

Women, for the most part, have been excluded from many kinds of experience—the armed services, competitive sports, high-level corporate or entrepreneurial life, as well as from leading roles in professional clubs and political offices—in short, most of the high-risk and high-visibility kinds of experience. The more that people participate in new areas of experience, the more they express their opinions and act according to what they think, the more they will trust themselves and build their confidence and ability to take on more active and significant roles. As they learn more about people and how they interact, about systems and how they function, they will increase their understanding of the world and hence of their own part in it.

We need to Experience Doing in order to overcome our limited conceptions of ourselves, conceptions that were formed during our childhood and as we grew up. Experimenting and trying on new behaviors allows us to redefine ourselves, to leave our past with its narrow and static views behind us. With experience we come to know and trust ourselves. Then success doesn't become an end in itself, an ultimate goal with tremendous fears related to it and on which we stake everything, but rather a *process of moving*.

# CHAPTER FIVE

# Risking Linking

*It is only by risking our persons from one hour to the next that we live at all.*
—WILLIAM JAMES

To *Risk Linking* is to take a leap into the unknown and accept the consequences. When we go out and meet new people, join a group or an association, or take a job in a field we're not familiar with, we take a risk. We may not get along with someone new; a community group or professional association may not meet our expectations; or we may find we don't like or are not suited to a new position. We're afraid we might lose something when in fact taking a risk many times over, trying something new, is vital to any successful career.

Risking Linking, then, is an exploration of new experiences with which we may not feel comfortable and secure. Risking Linking is also a search for a concrete opportunity, a new direction, a sense of belonging. In seeking out new experiences we are experimenting with ourselves and our sense of place in the world, our ability to meet each situation with ease and confidence. Risking Linking is a part of successful careering, but it is most noticeably practiced when there is a need for change in professions, in goals, in locations.

A highly rated newswoman at a Southern TV station decided to move to Los Angeles and look for new beginnings. To support herself and three teenage daughters when she first arrived, she worked as a secretary for a public relations firm. She did her job well, but without much enthusiasm, making no contacts that would open a door to the TV industry. Through a friend, however, she heard about an opportunity to work with a politically ori-

ented foundation. There was no salary but there was an
opportunity to make contacts with corporate sponsors.
Here was a gamble: three months' investment of time and
energy, foregoing salary, to apply media methods to social
issues with only the hope that some contact would pay
off for her. She decided to gamble, applied, and was accepted. It was soon after this that she came to me to talk
about her situation.

At first, she said, she was surprised at how ambiguous
and arduous the assignments at the foundation were.
Then she made the ultimate confession. She didn't want
to express her opinions and get very involved with her
colleagues for fear of revealing her ignorance of political
theory. She let others take initiative while she worked qui-
etly in her corner, doing her job well, but keeping her
ideas to herself. I urged her to use this opportunity to
develop herself and to try to resolve her reasons for feeling hesitant. After all, what terrible thing could happen?
Nothing, she agreed. She might even discover that she
knew more than she thought.

Her next assignment from the foundation was to write
a booklet with three other people for a sponsoring corporation. What happened is classic. The other three writers fell short; first they couldn't and then they wouldn't do
their parts. We considered her alternatives: she could stop
work too and hope that the others would come through
(which was unlikely); she could complete her part of the
job, which would show up the others but would still leave
her with an incomplete book; she could do the whole
thing halfheartedly and represent everyone at a mediocre
level; or, finally, she could turn out a spectacular job herself. She chose the last alternative. Then we discussed
whether she should take sole credit, give herself top bill-
ing, or make everyone an equal participant. She again
chose the last alternative. And she wrote an excellent
booklet which caught the eye of the corporate president.

After the work for the foundation ended, she was offered and she accepted a temporary job with a political
campaigner who was well known and highly respected.
She devoted all of her energies and skills to enhancing the
candidate and ensuring good publicity for him. What she
did not know was that her campaign manager and the
corporate president for whom she wrote the booklet were
good friends. She had unwittingly made a crucial connec-

tion. The manager touted her skills so highly that the president finally created an executive position for her in his media department.

How can we explain her success? Her friends said that it was a fluke, that she lucked out. Or you could say that she got the job because she was good—and she was surely more than good. But being good at something is only half the battle. Many competent people are working at jobs far below their abilities because being good is only half of what is required to be an Achiever. The other half lies in that triple-header—Self-Presentation, Positioning, and Connecting. She had practiced the first part, Self-Presentation, all her life, but she was without Connections in this new city. It was her willingness to take a gamble on Positioning and Connecting that made her successful.

Her effort to Risk Linking demonstrates the second of the Critical Career Competences. Like any other kind of skill, Risking Linking requires practice and study. While we can understand the Linking part of Risking Linking, which was critical to her success, it is harder to see the Risking part of that skill. Risking entails braving the fears of failure and rejection that arise when we start a new venture. For example, our former anchorperson was afraid of both rejection and failure. She was afraid that the foundation wouldn't want her and that if it did take her on, it would "find her out," that is, reveal her to be the fraud she too often felt herself to be.

We all fall prey to that fear, probably because we have more book-learning skills than life experiences. Cramming for two nights before a geology final and coming up with the highest grade makes us feel fraudulent when we might not be able to identify one rock pile from another a year later. Next to our own poverty of experience, we insist that an expert is an expert. We believe that we should be perfectly wise and prepared and are therefore terrified to start anything without being so. We forget that we will learn along the way, which is ultimately the way everyone gains knowledge and expertise in any area.

My client also had the completely opposite and simultaneous fear that the foundation might not be what it promised to be. Suppose her gamble fell through because the foundation failed to provide the situations and connections that would help her find a paying job. Then, too, suppose that by committing herself to a three-month program she would have to pass up any good offer that came her way. Not being able to be in more than one place at one time is a real opportunity cost, because by making a choice you must give up something else that might have been valuable to you.

She did not play her cards well at first. She didn't make a special effort to meet people in the television industry and then was almost ready to throw away her chance to make a place for herself in the political foundation. At one point she sabotaged her own ambitions to make contacts with corporate sponsors through her work at the foundation. Doing what she really wanted was tough, particularly for a woman used to "keeping step" rather than "stepping out." Her Risking Linking—her gamble—worked. It always works, but hardly ever are the details known in advance.

The most profound question next to "Who am I?" is "What do I want?" And, interestingly enough, both of these questions become clear only by experimentation. There is no way to know beforehand.

Our career decisions typically are made in high school or college—times when we have little or no real work experience and can only imagine what work is, based on secondhand information or on our parents' hopes for us, which are often a projection of their own unrealized dreams. Our options are thus limited by our inexperience and by the external definitions of work that are forced on us. We make crucial life decisions before we are truly able to evaluate our experiences and make our own critical judgments.

We also limit ourselves by adhering to an orderly and linear plan: first education, then work, finally retirement. This plan contradicts the behavior of successful people, which is characterized most often by movement back and forth between jobs and schooling or training, which shows an interest in several fields at once.

Let's look at our first misconception. We believe that if we go to the right schools and take the right curriculum we are guaranteed a prestigious career. Wrong. When I interviewed successful lawyers who had graduated from top-rated law schools (Harvard, Yale, Michigan, Stanford, for example), I also thought that automatically they had had connections with the best law practices. Yet many of them said that this was not so. They recalled their uncertainty about what kind of law to practice, and hadn't known whom to contact or even how to approach people when they went out to look for their first jobs. They did not know how or where to begin at all. There is no longer clear evidence to support the belief that an elite college and a prestigious professional school are a sure ticket to success.

In studying the lives of these successful lawyers who graduated from the best and the worst of law schools, I came to the conclusion that a professional school is often only a holding period. The years of law school constituted the only period in which nothing else happened in the lawyers' lives. They simply went to school and studied. Some married, which altered their social lives. But literally nothing else went on in their lives. There were no connections to lawyers in the larger community, nor to anyone in business or the arts. Such isolation is a regrettable waste of time and opportunity and is, I believe, encouraged by the system. The exceptions to this "rule" of isolation demonstrate the truth of the Risk Linking concept. The few exceptional students later used their outside ties to catapult themselves into desirable situations and considered the school's connections a rich resource throughout their careers.

Let me cite an example to demonstrate that Risking Linking in school is crucial. I asked one successful lawyer to tell me about his experiences as a contributor to *Law Review*. Invitations were offered only to those students standing highest in a class; *Law Review* certainly provided opportunities for recognition. But it had to be more than that. I asked exactly where he did his work for *Law Review*—in his apartment, at the library, or at the *Law Review* office. He said that at first he worked at the library because it was the most efficient, but then he realized that he was missing the whole point of working on the *Review*—the stimulating exchange of ideas with his co-professionals. So he began to work only at the *Law Review* office to overcome the anonymity and isolation that exists in a high student-to-faculty ratio. Very soon professors who before this time hardly knew him stopped in the office to talk about cases or problems, discussions that eventually led to personal friendships.

In another case, a young stockbroker new to her job was unhappy about the particular demands of her work. Although she claimed to be good with people, she could not bear telephoning strangers "cold," and trying to sell them something they might not want. After a six-month training program and four months on the job, she was convinced that she had chosen the wrong field. When I asked what she fantasized about doing, she answered, "Opening a successful boutique." She imagined that she could be friendly and nonaggressive with her clients in a beautiful, soft environment. I asked her how she would feel about encouraging her clients to buy what would both profit her and make them feel and look better, and if she could take advantage of the fact that many of us really do want to be sold something that we believe will enhance our image of ourselves. Immediately she realized how inappropriate her fantasy was and that what she was craving in her present dilemma was a safe, ego-nourishing place.

Smart as she was, she was making the same mistakes that are made by most young people new to work. Most people who cannot identify their specific skills say that they're good with people and assume that therefore they can sell. This assumption is false. Selling requires active persuasion of others. You must be willing to get people to buy things or services that they at first may not want or need. Although you may like the repartee, it is not a social event. Because you have to be able to take many rejections for every success, it requires great ego strength.

Our stockbroker agreed to stay where she was for a while and try Risking Linking. I asked her to find someone to team up with in that particular office, someone who would help her. She wondered why anybody would want to help her when they had their own profits to attend to. I suggested a trade—offering her ideas about how to do research, her strong suit, in exchange for help in another area. She agreed to ask other brokers about their experiences making "cold" phone calls, how they felt about them, what approaches they used, what worked and what didn't.

In doing this she learned a great deal. She also gave the other brokers a chance to show off their knowledge and thus to become fully conscious of what they knew. Nobody ever understands a process as much as when he or she teaches it to others. (You'll find more on the mentor-protégé relationship in Chapter Eight.) The stockbroker did, in fact, find a broker buddy and traded her research skills for his coaching on telephone calls—a business marriage of convenience that has launched her career.

Like the stockbroker, most of us think the only reasonable solution to our present career unhappiness is to quit immediately. We dream of running from A to B, conceiving of B as surely better. But I find from my own experience and that of many others that fleeing is a great mistake in most instances. Think for a moment of Job A, which represents what we want to leave, and Job B, that which we seek. Typically, because we feel closed to any more possibilities within Job A, we end up operating on the lowest level, pulling in and limiting ourselves. To move to Job B directly at this time is only to move horizontally, when we're feeling low and in search of an escape.

Fortunately there is an alternative to this kind of career suicide. I coach people to get all they can out of Job A, to develop their capabilities in a known situation. Job A is now low risk; there isn't anything that anybody can do to hurt you because you are going to leave soon anyway. Therefore, if you can take advantage of that situation to develop more of what you need, or choose one or two negotiations to push for, then you begin to build greater skills for yourself. You end up teaching yourself to be more powerful, so that when you do move to Job B, it is a different situation because *you* are different. As a result of the new attitudes and relationships you have developed at Job A, you see Job B's opportunities differently.

Risking Linking is hard to do, especially if you think it is cheating to rely on others. Consider another young woman who came from a distinguished old-line family. She determined to make it on her own, shunning the contacts under her very nose. Needing to start somewhere, she chose art education and worked her way up to be an administrator of a large art institute. When we analyzed those daily tasks which actually pleased her, we discovered to her complete surprise that they had nothing to do with art or administration but rather with realizing profit. She had a strong business sense that she had altogether discounted.

With this new information, she agreed to use her family's connections in banking and finance. Starting with her father and his friends, she scheduled appointments with each of them to talk about entering their fields. Happy to help, each one opened up entire networks where not only was my client well received, she was offered excellent starting positions. One offer was as a recruiting officer in the personnel department of a large bank, another was as a trainee in research analysis, leading to selling stocks and bonds. We agreed that the second position offered much more—connections and training in research, sales, and management. She had learned to put aside her old ideas of purity and independence and instead, through Risking Linking, embraced the world of alliances.

It can be very difficult to allow ourselves to Risk Linking. It means a willingness to move from the Sustainer's system of obedience and dependence to the Achiever's system, which combines technical competence with that elusive other half—the nontechnical skills.

Let me give you another example in which a refusal to Risk Linking nearly ruined a gifted actor's career. This client was an actor who had achieved great acclaim in his early work. But because of personal problems, he later left the social and work scenes familiar to him. Coming back to acting at a midpoint in his life had been courageous but difficult. Risking Linking promised the greatest likelihood of getting any work at all, but it meant that he had to take the chance of connecting again with a variety of people in show business. Besides the usual agent, manager, old friends, and supporters, I knew he still needed to have direct access to others who were essential to his success.

I began by asking him to list his everyday activities over the past two-week period. It was obvious that he did not go to any parties or social gatherings where contacts normally flourish. When I asked him why he avoided socializing, he irately slammed his fist on the table and said that he felt too awkward. I encouraged him to find four parties during the coming two weeks and go—not as himself, but as a character he could invent, or a character he had once played, or as another actor whose social skills he admired. By stepping into a role which he knew very well how to do, he would be forced to concentrate on something other than his fears.

He did try these things and discovered, of course, that he could go as himself; that is, as his best self—the self that he would like to show more of, the social, interactive, energetic, thoughtful, curious self rather than the self that was defensive, afraid, insecure, and retreating. Being more social made him realize that he could contact people he already knew in show business without hesitation. For example, he called one director with whom he had worked some time before and not only asked him to consider him for any new parts but, more importantly, spoke to him as a colleague, a friend. The director confided that he needed support, which he wasn't getting from his staff, and was relieved to find it in this actor. Then in his new role as "people broker," the actor introduced the director both to a lawyer whom he had just met and to a producer who had just reappeared in his life. He was beginning to shape his own opportunities.

Risking Linking extends beyond connecting with others for further contacts. It is also a means for establishing a reputation and it works for anyone—artists, professors, doctors, metallurgists, clerks, teachers, and bankers. Let's stay with bankers for another example.

A bank loan officer wanted to set up his own business, using his experience to answer a need that banks have failed to meet—helping small-business owners to expand by borrowing money. He took a part-time consulting job with one firm while he began to build his own clientele. Quite obviously he needed contacts. The loan officer was advised to offer a course at his neighborhood adult high school on how to use bank loans. This kind of teaching is not inherently profitable, but it is an extremely valuable opportunity to build a reputation and make contacts.

He was also to look for other ways to promote his new venture. Opportunities abound if only you are looking. A small-business convention was being held and I suggested that he attend and that at the end of the meeting he invite those who would like to continue talking to stay on for a drink. He was to learn to take advantage of people's real needs—to talk, to meet, to learn, to teach, to have an impact on others. He might also introduce himself to the sponsors of the convention, compliment their successes, make a few suggestions as to what else might follow, and even offer his services for the next time around.

Most of us attend professional conventions without attending to such personal needs. One personnel officer in charge of career development in a large organization attended two conventions within a month's time and had two entirely different experiences. The first was a great disappointment because none of the speakers, panelists, or topics added any new materials to that which he already knew. Feeling hopeless, he left early as he had done at past conferences, falling into the old trap of waiting for things to happen to him. Luckily, he had a second chance at the next convention to change his own behavior and to "happen to things." At the end of the first day's familiar agenda and rhetoric, he stood up and invited those participants interested in career development to meet for a drink. Only two men joined him, but they had national reputations in the field. Subsequently they invited him to join their task force, which worked on a continuing basis to redefine and build programs for career development. He had learned to Risk Linking in order to connect himself to ideas and people, establishing himself in a new network in a new field.

Many people are afraid to piggyback on a good idea. We pretend that the invention of new concepts and ideas is all-important. In reality, we also need to have a sense of building, monitoring, modifying, maintaining. Yet none of us is trained to build on anybody else's idea. We think that not only do we diminish ourselves by it, but we also take away from the other person's idea. Yet that is not so.

Robert Schrank of the Ford Foundation, formerly a

labor organizer, emphasizes the necessity of reinventing the wheel to find your own spin-off. By fearing to reinvent, you throw away all chances to invent. Building is enhancing. Rodin wrote, "I invent nothing; I rediscover." You don't steal the other person's ideas; you add to them, and by giving credit to the inventor or originator you acknowledge his or her creativity. Not to take up an idea out of fear is a real and significant loss. Remember that one aspect of success is the creation of opportunities, not only for oneself, but for many other people. Risking Linking is a first step.

Consider the case of a young lawyer in an outlying community who came to see me because of his self-imposed isolation from other lawyers. I suggested that he first Risk Linking to others by systematically introducing himself to them over lunch, one or two at a time, getting names and numbers from friends or from a professional directory. Later he could narrow his search to private-practice lawyers, or any lawyer he could meet at a Bar Association dinner. He needed to become active and to experience working with other professionals. He could also consider joining a civic or professional organization whose interests meshed with his. I recommended that for the next two months he read the local papers for the names of lawyers in the news and that he then contact them to express his appreciation of their efforts.

This young lawyer soon found other lawyers—some who needed his expertise, some who were peers. He called a meeting to talk about mutual problems, about the difficulty of finding clients and, more essentially, about the need to support one another. He was surprised to learn that many of his new contacts had longings similar to his. He ended his isolation by Risking Linking. It works because it is a system based on human contact.

When you're not sure what you want to do next but feel that you need new experiences and opportunities for growth, you can Risk Linking by making a lateral move within your organization. Lateral moves are often critical to successful careering. Such moves involve a great deal of risk but often open up many new possibilities. A department shift adds to your repertoire, giving you more options in the future; provides you with access to more people; and makes you more promotable as a manager, since you have a working knowledge of a variety of systems or processes.

I am circumspect about how much Risking Linking I assign to any client. With some, I suggest smaller, lower-risk plans and wait to see how well they work, while with others I pull out all the stops.

One young woman, with a year of advertising sales behind her, came ready to compete on a national scale. I, too, thought she was ready. I told her to gamble with her six-hundred-dollar bank account and buy a round-trip ticket to New York to go after the major client she wanted—*as practice for careering*. We refined and rehearsed her presentation until she was comfortable with it. Then we planned an alternative procedure in case the first one didn't work. I advised her to practice establishing links with other individuals, to use every chance she had to engage people in lively conversations, on the plane, in the hotel—in short, everywhere.

She returned from New York triumphant. Although she was refused by the first major client, she went immediately to Plan B. She had seized every opportunity to practice Risking Linking. She talked to fellow passengers and, surprisingly, not only had a good time but got an additional magazine lead; she engaged a stranger at a breakfast counter in a conversation and got still another publishing contact. She presented herself to the client she had come three thousand miles to meet and realized that they were wrong for each other. Then giving up what had been a year's dream, she aggressively contacted ten other potential clients, including her two new leads, and signed with seven of them within three days. One year later, she reports a booming business with more ideas and clients than she alone can handle, an affiliation with several important advertising associations, and an emerging national reputation. Because she was willing to Risk Linking, she had made exciting progress in her work.

Consider your own situation—whether you are moving up to a first-line supervisory level, already supervising and moving up to middle management, or ready to break into the limited top ranks from middle management. Let's assume that to get either the promotion or a raise you have to exhibit that set of skills needed to do the next job, even before you get to do it. Let's call it getting reclassified instead of being promoted.

A higher position really means more responsibility—taking charge of a project so that it is completed on time and within budget; motivating the project staff; resolving conflicts and solving endless problems. The real test comes not when things are going well, but when they aren't, which is surprisingly often. Doing well in responsible positions means getting done what must be done. But that is not all. Remember those non-technical skills used by Achievers.

## Practicing

To start, practice Risking Linking in safe environments —associations, clubs, or organizations other than where you work. The risk, believe me, is less real than imagined. Hardly anyone is ever expelled from a voluntary association. Professional, philanthropic, and civic associations are fertile ground for developing skills. First, of course, you must make yourself join. Then you must seize the opportunity to practice those skills you need, by getting involved in the various activities of the association, by speaking out and taking action. There are countless positions to try for. While most of us get stuck as a paying spectator, we could make ourselves do more—chair a committee, run for office. Positions like these develop our ability to negotiate, organize, delegate responsibility, motivate others, and, in short, to lead.

Then there's that old line to attend to—"It's who you know, not what you know." People in a variety of positions, each a part of a different network, become increasingly important to you. With them you begin to create your own network. While working together to promote and develop your organization you can build strong, long-lasting relationships. Perhaps one of the reasons that so much business is conducted over lunches, while golfing, or on business trips is that the normal "official" environment is changed, and therefore an implicit personal evaluation of one another is possible. A less charged atmosphere gives you a chance to discover your ability to relate comfortably on a social level and ultimately to do business together.

Risking Linking works when you want to change, whether or not you know the next step. And though change can be an extreme reaction, like that called for in the Sixties—banker to basket weaver—it can also be a viable alternative. But we must watch ourselves carefully, because often our dissatisfaction with what we expect to be the inevitable outcome of our career traps us into thinking that we want the extreme opposite. If we are feeling too dependent on any system, we want ultra independence. If we are feeling too competitive, we want only simplistic harmony. These are not choices but reactions, and therefore are not representative of who we really are. They carry a built-in doom.

Don't get me wrong. Failure in itself is not bad. In fact, as Dr. Marilyn Kourilsky, professor of Economic Education at UCLA, has found in her national studies, those children who grow up to be successful are those who experiment with the systems they have at hand, even if they initially fail. It is their persistent, repeated efforts to try any approach until something works (because they believe in and bet on themselves) that becomes their strength. The children who ultimately fail are those who perceive no alternatives, and when their project doesn't work, they leave it, grasshopperlike, for another. An important lesson lies with the children who believe they can make it work one way or another.

Kourilsky's findings support my own. Those successful lawyers whom I interviewed who made career changes tried a variety of situations to see if they would work. That language is critical: it was the *situation* that would work or not; it was never a direct test of themselves. And, when a situation didn't work, and it frequently didn't even after a couple of different approaches, they said, "It didn't work out." They were psychologically free to move on to something else that interested them, instead of branding themselves as failures and giving up. Although the risk may have been high, it was not perceived as life or death. But all too often failed experiences leave many of us emotionally pained, even paralyzed for a while. The reasons for this emotional reaction are disappointed expectation, an unrealized dream, and our internalization of the failure—we believe we have failed. This last reason is common to women, who tend to be less secure in the business world than men, and whose self-concepts are generally lower than men's. To pull ourselves up from feeling below standard, we need to experience many more situations, take more risks, and carefully observe what happens. Then we will learn to manage our reactions and keep pace with reality.

Although the ancient Greek, Heroclitus, wrote that "Nothing is permanent except change," change itself has only recently been studied. Donald Schoen, in *Beyond the Stable State,* posits that although we need change we search for stability—that we also need to be familiar with the tasks required in jobs and with the physical as well as the technical or interpersonal aspects. Then, if we are living our lives in a vital way, we need to grow beyond that secure, familiar state to another higher, more satisfying, challenging state. The time between the one and the other is always turbulent, fraught with doubt, ambiguity, anxiety. I have found no shortcut through this turbulent field; knowing about it beforehand helps to identify the pain but does not alleviate one bit of it. The only consolation is that once the decision is made to proceed, there is no going back to the same place.

Some quick cautions I give to clients who are exploring new careers: (1) don't take the first job offered, even if a month's search gets extended to three; (2) don't consider any job offer as an ultimate choice but rather as a transitional choice. This thinking will help you to avoid feelings of failure if you become dissatisfied with the new job after you have made a change.

When you are exploring a new area, make a systematic investigation and follow every lead. Record your contacts and their suggestions, taking notes on something you can keep—on extra-large Rolo-dex cards, three-by-five cards, or in a spiral notebook, with each name and address on one side and advice and notes on the back. In the massive search ahead, there is no possible way to recall who suggested whom, what you've promised to send, or even what you said and did.

If somebody gives you a name, suggesting a lead, then you have an obligation to reciprocate. There are numbers of ways to thank people, and I think one of the best is to report back to your original contact with the results of their suggestions, even if nothing particularly important took place. One client who had followed up on a friend's leads and gotten no good responses called his influential friend back to thank him and to ask for help in rehearsing his spiel, since nobody responded well. The friend took even more interest, helped him prepare a solid presentation, and then personally arranged some introductions.

One good turn does, in fact, deserve another, if not now, then later. You should never forget people who have helped you. It is not that you should think of direct repayment, but you should be aware of an implicit agreement—the absence of which makes us especially aware of its importance. When we go out of our way for others who do not show their appreciation, it dampens our giving the next time. Then, too, when we are in better positions, we can remember those who helped us by recommending them for panels, getting them media publicity, or even by being direct and asking, "How can I repay you now for what you did for me then?" I personally have had several opportunities to do this, chances that in the repaying enriched me as well as my benefactors. I have also received a variety of grateful reports.

One woman who had participated in a seminar that I had given some months previously wrote to me about her progress. She had taught high school math and physics for fifteen years before she left teaching. She saw it as a dead end and had turned down an opportunity to become a high-school principal. She wanted a job in industry, but had little idea of a way in. When she saw a Women-in-Engineering Fellowship Program advertised, she jumped at the chance, using her savings to support herself while taking this opportunity to get the special training she needed; it was her first effort at Risking Linking, which we had talked about in the seminar. When she later took her first good job, she also was willing to think of it as a transitional or intermediate step, rather than as final security, a notion that had been detrimental to her chances for mobility in the past.

Another client came to me with a curious dilemma. At the time she was doing publicity for a traveling show. As she traveled quickly throughout the country, through small towns as well as large cities, she was unable to cope with her loneliness. Because she traveled ahead of the show, she didn't even have the companionship of its members. Her only alternative, she thought, was to leave the company, but she had no connections with any other business. When I asked her whether she had occasion to engage in conversation other than shop talk with the newspaper, TV, and radio people she dealt with as part of her business, she said no. In all the innocence of her twenty-eight years, she revealed that she didn't "mix business with pleasure."

I immediately thought of all the sales and p.r. people traveling, isolated and lonely, following that nonsense dictum of not mixing business with pleasure. *Business is pleasure.* It is a mistake to think that there's anything but a mix. I therefore suggested that she make dinner dates with the media people she worked with, ask them about their jobs and their other interests, and thereby begin to build up a network of people and ideas.

I asked her to find a national organization to join so she could have chapters to visit. She was also at the time considering taking an M.B.A. An alternative college, a college without walls, might allow her to do a thesis that would entail interviewing people across the country, something with which she was very familiar. I thought the degree a good idea; it would open up many new career possibilities, connect her to new people and places through the interviewing, and, most important of all, force her to boldly embrace life.

I have found no other way to live life, let alone work, except to engage in it heartily. It is next to foolish to think that opportunity will come through an advertisement in a newspaper, though we all, employers as well as employees, secretly crave such magic. One C.P.A. firm was looking for an accountant who would be partnership material. They advertised in the newspaper. I urged them instead to be aggressive in their search by calling different clients for good candidates. In other words, I advised them to act as an executive search firm would act. What they clearly did not want again was someone who just needed a job. They already had him and were in the process of firing him.

People who answer ads in the paper, or use any other of the dependent "good student" systems, are very different people from those who use personal networks. The ones who use the network are much the stronger, for they demonstrate their willingness to take chances and to participate in a positive human system.

Risking Linking, like the rest of the Critical Career Competences, works best if you invest wholeheartedly in the process. You need to appreciate other people's time. You need to care about their work. You need to value people's stories and experiences, for they are the stuff of life itself, and can lead you to some of your own most rewarding experiences.

# CHAPTER SIX

# Showing Belonging

*She only loves who shows her love.*
—SHAKESPEARE

Successful people *Show Belonging* as second nature—virtually without noticing that they are doing it. If asked "What did you do today?" they simply respond with a list of their activities: I wrote a proposal; I worked on the project; I went to meetings; I settled a grievance. This list invariably omits the ordinary, everyday, minute-by-minute ways accomplished people have of doing things and most significantly their way of relating to colleagues, clients, and other work-related contacts. These people Show Belonging in the way they answer a call, talk with a staff member, and discuss a problem in a meeting. They send congratulations to a colleague who has published an article or won a case, or hold strategy meetings with their staff. Through acts of solidarity, cooperation, and enthusiasm, successful people Show Belonging.

People also Show Belonging by asking for support from others. During a seminar I ran for an international corporation, I asked one employee why she thought she was nominated to be manager of a new team. She could only suggest that she was chosen because her team thought she could do the job. When I next asked the woman who nominated her the reason for her choice, she smiled. She smiled for a long time. She finally explained that in another situation she would have said she based her choice on demonstrated merit and a sense of potential. Then she confided, "It was really because this woman sought me out. She had dinner with me last night and she asked my advice and even complimented my style. Since I have to say it out loud, it's because I think she's smart. And, of course, I think she's smart because she thinks I'm smart!"

The nominator admitted that she in turn liked the new manager's style. It probably wasn't very different from her own. She clearly responded to the manager's determination and energy. Of course she would never have made the nomination if she had thought for a minute that the younger woman was incapable of doing the job. But simply being capable of doing the job would not have produced the nomination. Being capable even might not have been noticed.

The younger woman did not seek out the other simply to secure a nomination. She genuinely wanted advice from this person whom she admired. In her eagerness and appreciation she Showed Belonging and she had an immediate result. It is important to understand, however, that Showing Belonging doesn't always yield such fast results. Through repeated efforts to be involved with others and to engage their interest in you, you can build a foundation of mutual support in your work situation which will be a continuing strength for you as you move in your career.

I learned some important things while working on a university research project. We wanted to find out if community service programs initially funded by the government were continued by the universities that housed the program offices after the federal funds ran out. If there were any programs in operation, we had to understand how they had survived. My research team first considered whether a particular community service project was in itself a good idea, whether it really did serve the community, and whether the project director brought in by the government to manage the project was competent.

As I went from institution to institution, interviewing administrators, faculty, and project staff, I came to realize that none of the above factors really counted. Although I personally valued some projects' purposes and methods more than others and preferred some directors over others, my own preferences did not correlate with what I discovered.

The single most critical factor was whether or not, and

to what extent, the project director Showed Belonging relative to the institution where the project was conducted. That is, the directors whose projects were continued were those who kept the associated departments and administration informed about the program's progress (through meetings, memos, conversations, etc.) and who credited the administration and/or faculty for their supportive efforts via media coverage (campus and city newspapers, radio, TV, etc.).

There were other directors who managed their projects well, and then waited for appreciation and a renewed contract. When it didn't happen they ended up self-righteous and bitter, expressed contempt for higher educational institutions and for the Department of Education in general, as well as for leaders whose projects were continued, for their "damned p.r. tactics," their "b.s.," and their "snow" jobs. Their attitude is supported by the belief that merit alone is what counts, despite much evidence to the contrary.

Showing Belonging and the next skill, Exhibiting Specializing, are complementary actions that we can take to shape our working relationships with others. They define the roles we choose within our working establishments, social organizations, and professional groups. These two complementary skills are the most important of the nontechnical skills used by Achievers. Yet, ironically, Showing Belonging and Exhibiting Specializing are also the most invisible. With practice they can help us form our best relationships with the people we work with and ultimately help us to reach our career goals.

It is important to most of us to experience unity and solidarity in our place of work. We are happiest when we sense a spirit of cooperation within our organization. At its best that spirit is like the give and take that exists between lovers who try to support and enhance each other as generously as possible.

Your relationships with the people you work with can be enhanced by a similar exchange of encouragement, admiration, approval. Every day presents opportunities to demonstrate our caring, but we seldom act on them. We are short on praise to our employer or colleagues for their work, and we suffer in return. Most of us would be satisfied with a simple "good job" or other brief acknowledgment; instead we get implied low-level criticism or simple indifference.

I recently gave a management training seminar for supervisors of construction units at a large utility. At the end of the first day I knew that I wasn't very popular with my audience. The second day the mood had not improved; many of the men didn't want to hear what I was telling them. Then, just as the seminar was about to end, one foreman spoke out. He realized that he had resisted my ideas because he hadn't wanted to admit his own responsibility for his failure to move ahead in his company. During his twenty years on the job, he had never spoken to his supervisor or anyone else above him except to report on his work. He never went out for lunch or for a drink with any of them; he never inquired about their families, their weekends, their vacations, and certainly not about their career goals. He now not only saw why he had not been promoted but also realized that his feelings of powerlessness had kept him from promoting deserving persons on his team. He thought of anyone who moved up or out as a traitor. He compensated for his passivity and fear by controlling the people beneath him and making it more difficult for them to advance themselves. He then explained that he was afraid of "brownnosing." He didn't want to appear to be using his position as a way to get to the more powerful people in the company.

Though this foreman's attitude was self-imposed, it is one that originated in our early school experiences. The desire to succeed in the classroom was often overcome by a fear of charming or manipulating our way to the teacher. Even a good student was criticized by his or her peers for being a "teacher's pet." We carry this idea into our work lives too often, and it works against us. We mistrust people who build good relationships with their superiors because we are reluctant to do it ourselves. It is imperative that we outgrow our childhood attitudes and fears and learn a new approach to careering. Showing Belonging is one part of this positive, active approach to our work.

A management consultant came to me to learn how to Show Belonging. This client isolated the particular skill he needed after he had heard me speak to an audience of consultants. He knew he was doing something wrong and he had proof—business was dropping off. He told me, for example, that he had once taught a course for a large management institute which drew an audience of personnel directors. Months later, one of the directors called the institute for both a repeat course and a follow-up. The institute, not having either to offer at the time, recommended that the director go straight to the instructor-consultant. The director did, but my client felt uneasy. Although he accepted the offer, he nonetheless felt as if he were cheating both his firm and the institute. Quite obviously he was not cheating at all; neither was he crazy or stupid for feeling that way. He was having trouble defining an appropriate way to get new business while continuing old business, a problem common enough to novice consultants.

What my client didn't realize is that he was limiting himself, his company, and the institute by not taking an obvious opportunity to Show Belonging. I recommended that he first contact the person at the institute who had acted as a broker for him and thank him. He looked astonished, never having thought of doing that. Then he could suggest that the institute offer the course again, and he might also suggest an idea for the second in a series of courses. I further encouraged him to talk with the personnel director to design the next training session to meet the director's company's needs.

Another management consultant came to me with an unusual dilemma. He was constantly being compared to his partner and found lacking. He didn't necessarily want to compete but rather to develop his own strengths. I asked for an example of some work they had done together to understand what he meant. Recently, he said, they were asked to help campaign for a friend running for a small elective office. His partner agreed to make telephone calls, canvassing three times a week until the election. It was a finite task which he did well enough to earn a service award months later when their friend won the election.

On the other hand, my client offered to manage one complete division of the campaign—a good-intentioned pledge but made cavalierly without taking into account the nature and requirements of his business. As a self-employed consultant, he was dependent on new business, and could not turn away any important contract that came his way. When one did come, he had to work hard and he couldn't act on his campaign pledge. Apologizing to his friend, he now offered to match his partner's contribution, canvassing three nights a week. But once you promise something big, you can't substitute something small and still win—and my client had some options he never considered. For instance, he might have done both jobs himself by working day and night. Or, he might have delegated work, even hired others to help manage the campaign or his contract.

At any rate, because he did perform a service for his politician friend, I asked him to tell me in detail how he actually went about the telephoning. He described the room, a large one with some smaller offices off to the side. Most of the volunteers worked in the middle of the large room at a phone pool. His partner sat with his co-workers and periodically asked them about the reactions they had had to their calls, which approaches worked with which types of people, and what surprises they had had. That he got the volunteers to share their experiences was, in my client's words, "pure bullshitting." He juxtaposed his own behavior, choosing instead to sit alone in one of the small offices where he made twenty times the number of calls that anybody else had made.

We have to consider what it meant, in this case, to do the job. Certainly the primary goal was to get voters to come out to vote for the candidate. But it was also important for the volunteers to share information that would help them to attain that primary goal. That sharing would also help them to feel involved and unified in a purposeful and important activity. My client's partner, consciously or not, understood the value for everyone of Showing Belonging. He knew that the volunteers could share information that would make them more effective and that by enhancing a routine task he would make them feel important.

My client, however, still believed he had done more and therefore better work, and in truth he had made more calls. But that is not all that working is about. To Show Belonging we have to validate, support, and enhance our work force, no matter whether it is labeled political, volunteer, or corporate. We must show identification with our co-workers and establish a relationship of mutual exchange and cooperation in our jobs. Once we have created this base of support—for ourselves as well as for others—we are able to take more risks, assert our individuality, and accept the individuality of others.

You can practice Showing Belonging in the ordinary events of your daily life by being considerate of others and by behaving as though you expect them to be considerate of you. Become a part of what is going on around you, whatever it may be in your job and in every other aspect of your life. We need practice in living and interacting. Nothing is too small or insignificant as a stage. Traditionally we have been taught not to talk to people unless we have been introduced or unless we wear some badge—a three-piece suit, an army surplus jacket, long or short hair. That says we also belong to their group. But this limits our experience.

At work you have a ready-made opportunity to Show Belonging. Think about what you do when you walk into a room. Whom do you greet when you come in? Only those for whom you work? Or everybody? Do you remember what's on each day's agenda so that you're ready to work? There are infinite ways of Showing Belonging in your work situation, but you can begin by acting as though you do belong. You might not truly feel that you do, but you must assume that you do and behave accordingly by making a contribution. Eventually you will feel comfortable, but only through participation and involvement. Say what you think, offer a suggestion, ask questions, show your interest and enthusiasm. Remember that there is no *one* right answer, and it can never hurt to try. Think of the people in your office who seem to belong in a way that you would like to, and ask yourself how they might handle a situation that's difficult for you. Watch them and imitate them. It may feel awkward at first, but you will find your own style. You will be trying on a new role, so give yourself the room to make mistakes. You will be surprised at your imagination and ability.

I think it is important to consider the differences between women and men in relation to these skills. While I have seen many successful people, both men and women, demonstrate them effectively, I believe that women in general find it more difficult to take risks, to demonstrate their talents, to ask for advice from authority figures, to take part in an active way in whatever they do. They tend to be more passive because they have not been socialized to be active or to speak out, though certainly there are exceptions. If anything, they've been taught to keep to themselves and not make known their wants or aspirations. In some ways I think the good student syndrome applies more often to women than to men, simply because men, as little boys and later, were allowed to do things and were taught things that were said to be not for women. Those things were taught in school, in the home, and in the general society: they add up to a greater feeling of independence and an ability to move through the world with ease. Only very recently has the whole world begun to be considered a place for women, whose roles as wives and mothers have been portrayed for so long as their primary roles, and sometimes as their only desirable ones. And because so many women are new at what they do—are just starting to build careers or are trying on roles they never dreamed of—they are more reluctant to get into the action. They have to make up for what they didn't get in the way of encouragement and support. But if they start at the beginning and build up their confidence, they will catch up with those men and women who have had a head start.

The skill of Showing Belonging is interesting in this regard. Women are expected to be, and usually expect themselves to be, supportive and caring of others. Accordingly, they are generally willing and able to share responsibility and to work with other people for a common goal. As a rule, they know how to cooperate with their co-workers—on a horizontal level, as I think of it, in terms of a corporate structure or any hierarchy. But they are not equally comfortable showing belonging to the larger organization, or to people above them—the vertical dimension. That requires a self-confidence that many women, even those who have achieved a measure of success in their fields, have yet to feel. Men, on the other hand, are more likely to be comfortable with their superiors, and to perceive themselves as part of the company as a whole. They are quicker to show their special talents, to Exhibit Specializing and make themselves unique. But because they are generally encouraged to be independent, even aggressive, cooperation is not as important for them as is individual achievement, sometimes at the expense of others. Thus they are not particularly good at Showing Belonging to people below them or even to their peers. Both men and women can benefit by using their strengths to the utmost, and by developing those aspects of Showing Belonging and the other skills with which they are least adept.

An engineer with whom I have worked recently reported a new breakthrough. As a supervisor in a paper-making machine company, she needed to find some ways of Showing Belonging to her all-male unit. She set aside Mondays to learn about and work with every machine, and she demonstrated to her workers that she could do their jobs. Soon they showed her a respect they hadn't felt before. They came to her with their requests for improvement in conditions and in the design of the machines themselves. She could take part in these discussions as a result of her new understanding and thus she extended her original, limited notion of supervising—from performing the task of overseer to being concerned with the workers' attitudes toward her and with their need for recognition. Because she got into the workers' role and invited them to participate in a managerial task, she made considerable progress toward a more effective, productive working relationship based on trust.

Look at your own organization. Whatever your situation is, if you had the power to fire, whom would you fire for not caring about the business anymore? And whom would you promote for operating for the general good? How can you apply these insights to help yourself to contribute more? We all know the importance of reciprocity. We will contribute more to get more. And if we don't contribute, we can't hope to get anything.

Often when we feel ignored or discounted in our jobs it is because we don't participate enough and don't understand that our lack of involvement is what prevents us from feeling satisfied. If we look closely at our behavior and realize our passivity, we can act to change it, to be more engaged, to take on more responsibility. Then when we do get rewards, when we are noticed and clearly appreciated for our efforts, we can see what we have done to make others respond to us. Of course, sometimes we don't realize what it is that we are doing when we *are* recognized. It doesn't occur to us that we've had a part in getting that recognition. If, however, we consider that those rewards are more than the result of chance, we can analyze what we have done to earn praise and we can learn from it. If we *show* people what we can do, they can't help but see and appreciate our abilities. Success demands that dual effort—opportunity-taking and -making. And Showing Belonging is the first step toward realizing those opportunities.

# CHAPTER SEVEN

# Exhibiting Specializing

*Every human being is intended to have a character of his own; to be what no other is, and to do what no other can do.*

—WILLIAM ELLERY CHANNING
(American Unitarian clergyman, 1780–1842)

This Critical Career Competence, Exhibiting Specializing, together with Showing Belonging, forms the core of the skills that successful people demonstrate in their careers. Although at first they might not seem to be, the two skills are actually complementary to each other and fit most importantly into the categories of Self-Presentation and Positioning.

As we have seen, Showing Belonging in your working environment emphasizes active participation, cooperation, and a spirit of solidarity with your co-workers. Rather than simply coming in on time, doing their jobs in a passive, mechanical way, and collecting their paychecks and benefits, successful people assert membership by sharing responsibility and working with others.

Exhibiting Specializing means developing and making accessible to others our unique talents. While in Showing Belonging we serve the needs of our organization by working for the total good, in Exhibiting Specializing we serve these same needs and fulfill our own needs by demonstrating our individual and special abilities. Both Critical Career Competences work as halves of a total personality. We need to learn to use both simultaneously.

Here are some brief examples of people who have found opportunities to Exhibit Specializing.

- A real estate developer seized an opportunity to write up an administrative code. At a crossroads in his life, he took a year and a half to contribute to his profession as well as take time to "find himself." By creating a systematic code he became the expert in a special area, gained a statewide reputation, and fulfilled a particular need of his profession.

- A city planner went beyond what was expected of her and earned a prominent place for herself by becoming her firm's "planner's planner." Members of several departments come to her as problem-solver, thinker, broker. What she actually does is not even hinted at in her job description. She has served her firm in a capacity that has continued not only to satisfy her abilities and needs, but also to greatly benefit the other workers on the staff.

- A young lawyer compiled a notebook of outstanding cases to be used as a model for young public lawyers. He set up a system citing precedents and alternative ways of thinking for the cases most often encountered. He not only helped others, he also displayed his talents for organization. His willingness to use his extra time for such a contribution to public law was not overlooked; no other lawyer in his department has advanced so quickly.

- An oil company administrator, herself an amateur painter, set up the first exhibition of corporate arts and crafts. Thus she created a new position in public relations for herself.

- A public lawyer used his previous expertise as a policeman to contribute to his office. Realizing that district attorneys were not getting enough information from policemen involved in narcotics cases, he spent hours of his own time drafting questions that would help to reveal what the police knew. His contribution was rewarded by his department and his work was genuinely appreciated by his colleagues.

Each of the people in the above examples found a way of Exhibiting Specializing in the context of his or her particular job. They each saw a need that was not being met and, at the same time, an opportunity to satisfy their own strivings. To Exhibit Specializing we must add to our regular responsibilities. The extra work that we do means extra time and effort for which we are not normally compensated. But for our investment of time and energy, for our commitment, we are compensated in a different way because we are more valued. And, to be sure, if we do not take it upon ourselves to develop and make known our special abilities, we will not advance in our jobs. Exhibiting Specializing is not the only skill we need to make progress, but it is a very important part of a career-enhancing approach to our work. Through this skill we learn more about ourselves, our interests and talents, and we reveal ourselves to the people around us. We must show who we are in order to be recognized and appreciated.

To know where to begin, look to those of your interests which can logically coincide with your work. For instance, two lawyers—a white woman and a black man—have used their uniqueness to respond to current needs in their jobs. The woman worked for women's civil and criminal rights in a large, prestigious firm. Her feminist legal activities, which take her outside her firm, have established her statewide reputation not only as a sex-discrimination attorney but also as a first-rate litigator. The black lawyer, in addition to his teaching and scholarly responsibilities as a professor of law, has begun counseling black law students. In this way, he acts as a role model for young blacks.

Both lawyers made the most of their professional situation; they too saw a need which they could answer, and in so doing used their special expertise and acted on their concerns. We can see Positioning at work here. Both lawyers took on added responsibilities, augmenting their status and expanding their area of achievement. In nearly every case I can think of, Exhibiting Specializing has meant extraorganizational, extracurricular, voluntary efforts. Recognition comes in time.

The following examples of Exhibiting Specializing are the experiences of several of my clients. They demonstrate the process that people must go through to understand how to Exhibit Specializing. Remember, it takes practice to do anything well.

An assistant to a national sales manager in a small communications firm wanted to upgrade his image. He had been underpaid to begin with, had not gotten a raise in two years, and was concerned about staying in the company. His job was to prepare customers for the sales-men; he did not get any commission and was not given credit for his work. He obviously had to change some-thing, and the most obvious opportunity for change is in the situation at hand. In his constant and fairly loose contact with potential customers, my client had been able to collect a great deal of important information. He had been able to discover, for example, what his clients really wanted, what the competition was doing, what program-mers promised but didn't deliver. He needed to get this information to the president, and he had to find an ap-propriate way to communicate it.

One effective way to pass on information (aside from the usual memo or report), especially applicable in this situation, is to tell an anecdote. I suggested to my client that he compose and rehearse short stories about the firm's clients and competitors. I urged him to practice pacing himself, to learn to tell a story in the time that he had to tell it. For instance, if he and the president were in an elevator, then his story had to be less than the time it takes to go up or down. If they were walking down the hallway, then his story had to be as long as the corridor is long. Comedians are not the only ones who must learn to develop great timing. Some of his anecdotes could be one-liners, others could be three minutes or ten minutes long. I wanted my client to invent ways to reveal what he knew, what he thought about the company, what his contributions and suggestions were. He agreed to practice this new behavior as a way to break out of his passivity and hoped that he would be noticed.

In the practice of Exhibiting Specializing, he also be-gan to believe in himself in a different way. And, as you would expect if you have done it yourself, other people began to believe in him, too. The latest report that I have had is that he got an unheard-of raise from his company and several higher offers from competing firms. He now faces the new dilemma of which one to choose—a problem of the best kind.

Opportunities to exhibit our talents and make contributions are everywhere. We have chances at every turn, even when we are starting something new. A researcher for a large corporation, eager to change his position, went on a number of interviews for a variety of jobs. I asked him to tell me what he told his interviewers about himself and he said that he went through his job history. He thought that this would best demonstrate his development and progress over the years. From an interviewer's point of view, however, this was not the best representation of his experience. His Self-Presentation tended to sound like a transcript of his job record, not like an evaluation of his talent and ability.

Many of us have made the same mistake; we are good-students-turned-job-seekers, telling our stories from A to Z. I told my client to consider some different strategies for Self-Presentation. For example, he could portray his abilities according to their field of application. Because he had worked on both housing and educational projects, he might compare the types of research he had done in each field and draw some conclusions about his findings. Or he could talk about the statistical analysis he had done and its application to several fields. He could also refer to his supervision of people working with certain kinds of statistics and research. In this way he becomes the designer of his past, instead of having it determine him.

We all have to interpret and shape our past work experience, depending on what each situation calls for. Our past contains much more than facts in chronological order. Yet to choose a chronological presentation is to represent ourselves as students and to empower our interviewers as teachers to look for shortcomings. By choosing ways to talk about our abilities and dominant interests in a general way, we offer a more sophisticated and compelling interpretation of our experiences and interests. If we think of our past as raw material, then we can shape and interpret it to our advantage and put our best self forward. We can become specialists in many different areas (as indeed many of us are) according to the position for which we are being considered.

Too often we act against ourselves. We are embarrassed by this kind of positive manipulation because it makes us sound "too good." We are therefore more likely to start from our earliest and weakest point to prove that we worked step by step up to the present. But it may be the least accurate description of who we now are—skilled, competent, aggressive, and imaginative. Good self-marketing is talking toward what the other person wants in terms of general ability, commitment, the desire to learn, personality, and so on. While bragging is offensive, revealing our abilities, interests, and unique talents is positive and captures attention and respect, and inevitably results in a job offer that we've been hoping for.

Often we feel inhibited about speaking out. I coach people to talk about their approaches to certain problems and the strategies they found most effective in a particular context. It's not enough to say "I'm good at X." It's important that we explain how and why by giving examples so that others will realize what our special abilities are, what we contribute, and why we would be right for the position in question. We can also talk about what we might do if we had to tackle a given problem a second or third time, which gives us a chance to reveal our knowledge of the field.

A professional interviewer who had been in one of my seminars during the past year called to tell me how exciting her new work assignment was. For her research on housing needs for the aged, she was conducting very successful interviews. Now it was time for her to consider her next strategic step, which would concern Exhibiting Specializing with a view toward getting her project refunded. Her interviewing techniques were original and could benefit others, like myself, who were frustrated by the lack of helpful guides to interviewing. I suggested that she begin Exhibiting Specializing by publishing articles on her techniques and experiments in research journals and in a textbook.

My client was reluctant to take what seemed like too big a step, so I encouraged her to act as an editor and find others to contribute articles on what they had learned about interviewing specific audiences—the aged, consumers, tenants, landlords, and so on. She knew that different audiences require different interviewing strategies and, in drawing together a body of information on effective interviewing, she was able to find a focus for her talents and Exhibit Specializing.

Often some of our most original or unique accomplishments go unnoticed, buried in the piles of papers and reports that our companies generate. That is why it is so important to make your work known to others and to find ways of making significant contributions. Try to pinpoint what the needs of your organization are; then plug in your special knowledge and talent. Let others know that there is a need that you can fulfill and you are on the road to success.

If you're thinking of changing jobs but don't feel quite ready to make a move, Exhibiting Specializing can help you to gain confidence, to practice critical new skills in your current job, and to prepare you for a change.

The dean of financial affairs of a university came to me to talk about a career choice. He could not decide whether to stay in academia, where he had security and some job satisfaction, but little influence in raising funds for student scholarships, or to change to entrepreneurial financial investing. Previously he had successfully sold real estate and could return to that or another related field, but it was not his first choice.

My first suggestion was for him to begin Exhibiting Specializing right where he was. Our goal was to get him more recognition on the campus with the faculty and the alumni and to increase his knowledge of, and association with, other financial fields. One way to start would be to coordinate and moderate a series of seminars on financial investing for both the faculty and professional alumni. He would meet with a variety of people who practiced financial management in various areas, learn about their work, and invite them to participate in the seminars. In this way he would make many contacts, gain information about work that interested him, and reveal his own knowledge and curiosity about financial management. In the process, he learned a great deal about himself and others and grew more confident about making a bridge to a new career in the financial world.

Another client, vice-president of a small, respected non-profit organization, was in a similar bind. He was not getting recognition for his work and thought it was time for a career change. Again I suggested that he consider opportunities at hand before making a drastic change. He agreed to rekindle old connections as well as make new ones. For example, he would build a better relationship with one member of the board of directors, who was also on the faculty of the local university, and ask him privately for some expert advice. With this man's assistance, he would eventually devise a new research program and draw attention to himself for his innovative ideas. He found a way to make use of his talent for designing and implementing procedures and discovered a new career in his present one. And he also learned that at times it's important to ask for help.

A personnel officer in a small organization faced a situation that we all have found ourselves in at one time or another: a too-smart person with a no-place-to-go job. When we listed problems that she might make into opportunities, she saw that there was an unusually high degree of turnover despite an exceptionally competent staff. Here was a chance to do something. Why not develop an orientation program that would reduce turnover? My client began by presenting to her director her idea for a study that would indicate whether or not such a program was warranted. Her aims were to become visible to top management, to demonstrate leadership to her director, and to design a program that would help the organization.

First she interviewed key people in the organization. She wanted to find out how they learned to perform their jobs, how they gained acceptance as newcomers, what kinds of problems they encountered as new personnel, and why they wanted to stay with the organization. We rehearsed different ways of asking questions and discussed how she could present herself in such a way as to draw the attention of her subjects. She accomplished what she set out to do. She compiled the experiences of her interviewees and developed a viable and sophisticated orientation program for high-level employees. She also gained the confidence of these executives and as a result had their invaluable support for subsequent, more substantial programs.

Some time later the personnel director asked my client,

for the first time, to reveal her long-range goals within the organization. She told him that she wanted more of everything—more status, more responsibility, more salary —but could not agree to pursue any one of the four programs he proposed as alternatives for her next project. She then proposed her own plan to develop and manage a new training program which she could expand according to the company's needs. Her work eventually brought her the kind of recognition she sought. The important lesson here is one of sensitivity to the work environment, which brings opportunities for self-enhancement into focus —opportunities that are realized through unique contributions and demonstrated ability.

Sometimes Exhibiting Specializing can enliven an otherwise thankless or boring task. A loan officer in the headquarters of a large bank had to deal regularly with faulty loan applications and forms incorrectly or inadequately completed by branch officers, which resulted in delayed processing. Her task was worse than routine; yet I knew there was a problem there somewhere that she could turn into an opportunity. After we talked she decided to compile a handbook of the most widely used loan forms and include fast, easy directions plus eye-catching graphics (which she loved to design) to point out the easily overlooked or misinterpreted parts of loan application forms. This handbook would showcase her special knowledge and, at the same time, make her job and the jobs of branch loan officers easier. By helping these officers complete forms more accurately and thereby expedite their customers' loans, she found a way to get recognition for her work, and to make contact with the other bank officers. Later she would go out to the branches to talk about her handbook and establish herself as a loan expert for the bank.

It's good to Exhibit Specializing in a new job right at the start. A new manager wanted to establish her own style, one that would distinguish her from her predecessor. She decided to institute a new data-processing operation. The change, unpopular just because it *was* a change, was going to be difficult to make. She immediately involved her staff by calling a meeting. She prepared her presentation carefully, and at the meeting asked her staff to make suggestions for a smooth changeover from the old to the new system. Then she analyzed the responses and drew up some plans. Later she thanked each person for his/her suggestions and showed each of them how their ideas were used, directly or indirectly. The support and respect she earned from her staff made her investment of time and effort an invaluable one.

Too often we hold ourselves back from demonstrating our talents and revealing our insights. Why do we hold back? Partly because we are afraid to appear too aggressive, too ambitious. And there is also the fear of being found out—are we really as smart as we hope? We probably are, but we sell ourselves short and withhold information that will promote us and benefit others. And though many of us shrink from the idea of packaging and selling ourselves, it's important to remember that, just as we can only appreciate what is made known to us—whether it is a product, an organization, or an individual—others can only appreciate us if we reveal ourselves to them, making known our abilities and interests. I coach people to do exactly that, to demonstrate their creativity and enthusiasm, their special skills and hidden talents.

# CHAPTER EIGHT

# Using Catapulting

*Our chief want in life is somebody who shall make us do what we can.*

—EMERSON

In the past many people learned their trades by apprenticing themselves to a master who demonstrated the required skills and gave them first the simpler tasks to do, later the more difficult ones. Eventually apprentices became completely independent, having reached the level of their master in expertise. At that time the masters placed them in other shops if they could not keep them. Vestiges of such a system still remain. Some young men, and more recently some women too, have been fortunate to have found "masters" or mentors to help them plan their careering steps, from the first to the next and on up the ladder until they are well on their way to the top. An experienced person can teach some of the most important skills, and in particular the nontechnical ones that I am most concerned with. This system of sponsorship has traditionally been for men, and only recently has it begun to include women who have, after all, only recently entered the professions and business in significant numbers. We still have a long way to go, and we can begin by realizing the importance of the mentor/protégé relationship and making it a part of our efforts to build a career. We can *use people in the best sense* to catapult us into situations or positions we could not otherwise reach, in the same way that a pole vaulter relies on the pole to enable him to reach his highest goal and catapult himself over the top. There are some things we can't do without a push to help us get where we want to go. But we have to learn to ask for advice and support.

*Using Catapulting* is a two-part skill which requires, first, the establishment of a significant relationship with a more experienced individual and, second, the carrying out of positive moves that are taught or suggested by the mentor. The second part is harder because it demands independent effort and active participation, which in turn are ultimately the best teachers. But many of the opportunities for taking risks and experiencing doing and making contributions begin with the mentor whose connections, expertise, and encouragement are invaluable and provide us with new ways to exercise and develop our abilities.

We are just beginning to collect lore about how people find and use mentors. In the modern organization mentors are a virtually untapped resource. Accounts from successful people who have been helped immeasurably by others show that the mentor-protégé relationship is an alliance which can be crucial to successful careering at the beginning and middle levels.

Mentors, like wished-for fathers and mothers, guide us in how we present, position, and connect ourselves. We want to know that we have someone in our corner to defend us against attack and help us plan our best strategies. Most often, our mentors work in the same field as we do, somewhere near the top. That usually means that they have moved up from within. So we count on their knowledge, not only of the work itself but, perhaps more important, of what it takes to make that climb. That knowledge can only come from years of dealing with people in a professional setting. The "politics" of the workplace are often very difficult to penetrate, and they dictate behaviors or attitudes that newcomers must learn, often through a painful process. Mentors can alleviate some of that pain by explaining the way a system functions and by giving us special clues that only veterans can know. They will often be able to foresee developments in our position before we do, perhaps because of privileged information regarding executive decisions, or because they can sense our strengths even before we do and can encourage us to take a big, new step, or they will introduce us to someone who will prove to be the next link in our advancing career.

Mentors are seldom our immediate supervisors or managers or even in our departments. If they were, they would have less objectivity. They wouldn't want to lose their really good people, nor would they want to be shown up in any way. The relationship between a boss and a subordinate is a difficult one, susceptible to the stresses of jealousy and competition and inequality. It is unlikely for a mentor/protégé relationship to be born there. A mentor must above all be someone you respect and admire and whom you think of as a model for your own career.

Some corporations, in the hope of creating a permanent, committed staff, have formalized a system of mentoring. They arbitrarily assign new young people to trusted high-level staff members. Whether such a forced relationship actually works depends on the two who are assigned to each other. One young engineer, paired with a proven manager, asked his advice on a specific problem. She was being offered a position as recruiter. An ambitious engineer, she was willing to move from the technical to the managerial track, but she had disdain for the job of recruitment. Her mentor, after having considered her case, strongly urged her to take it for a year and to work hard. Her future with the company depended on some demonstrated sacrifices like this, he told her. She followed his advice and then discussed with him the opportunities inherent in her new situation. He told her that she had been the object of jealous talk, and counseled her on how to protect herself from people who might try to make trouble for her. He also made a list of her supporters and explained how she might make more of their support, by encouraging them to come to her for help and by simply talking to them. He told her how she could get herself in line for a promotion, and suggested a series of moves that would broaden her managerial experience. She could never have progressed so well alone. No one could have.

Using Catapulting implies a relationship between us and those significant others who, in our opinion, are more experienced, more knowledgeable, and more extablished in their organization or profession than we are. Because they are the experts, it is natural for them to attract many people who wish to use them as the poles which will Catapult them to success. But Catapulting via a mentor is a give-and-take situation. We do not take without giving something back. The mentor/protégé relationship is informal, even personal, and not bound by time. Because we share our mentors' connections and experiences, because we are being given entrée into their world, we become a reflection of them. Therefore we need to be aware that by our excellent performance we are enhancing our mentors. There are, of course, other considerations too. As your relationship with your mentor is not formed by explicit contract, you must approach him or her with respect and a sense of proportion. You cannot ask for advice about everything, though you may fervently wish to do so. You must be selective and consider which moves or strategies concern you the most and about which you are the least secure. You can't ask someone to act in your place, or tell you precisely what to do at every moment; you don't want to present yourself as a patient or a student in the passive "do for me" mode. It's also best not to complain about other people or missed opportunities but to maintain a positive attitude.

A mentor is someone who can help you to solve work-related problems in areas where you feel inhibited by your inexperience. Perhaps you want to suggest a different emphasis on a project, but you're not sure how to make your presentation most effective; you want to present your findings, but you're not sure what to stress. A mentor can help you evaluate a possible career move so that you make a careful, reasoned decision. And if you're not sure what is an appropriate behavior in a new situation, a mentor can give you crucial guidance—in how to ask for a raise, how to negotiate for more time on a particular assignment, or how to set up a meeting you think is necessary. A mentor can show you how business gets done, and business can mean a wide variety of exchanges and transactions. And perhaps most important, you might find some project, committee, or other activity where you can work together with your mentors to learn firsthand what *moves* are appropriate in various situations.

As a protégé you have an implicit obligation to your mentor to act on his or her advice and to report back on the results of your actions, especially if you are successful. Mentors want to know how their advice has helped you and they are delighted when you show your enthusiastic appreciation of their efforts.

Of course a mentor's advice will not always work; it's very unlikely that it would in every case. But when it doesn't, don't give up on your mentor. Explain what happened; ask for comments, more advice, and suggestions for alternative moves, and don't forget to show your appreciation. Later on, when you are operating from a new, more powerful base, you may be in a position to repay your mentor with valuable contacts or new clients.

A prominent lawyer I know began his legal career as a bailiff in the court of a judge he greatly respected. One day he asked the judge to help him make an important decision. Should he go to law school and which would be a good school? He told the judge how much he admired the way he tried his cases. The judge responded warmly to the young man's request, and told him he thought law would be a fine choice of career. Then he strongly recommended him to his best friend, the dean of a reputable law school that scheduled night classes. The bailiff continued his relationship with the judge during the years of his schooling, received guidance about electives, about the types of public law to practice, and finally about how to move within the field.

Most Sustainers cannot bring themselves to use a mentor to Catapult their careers upward. Instead, as I have said before, they insist that hard work and merit alone count, and they believe that to use others is cheating, though I think that it is fear that keeps them isolated, a carry-over from the good-student syndrome. What they don't realize is that asking for advice and then acting on it is the supreme compliment that one can give another person. Sustainers deprive themselves of the Achiever's expertise and keep themselves entrenched in their one job or position. Sustainers also believe that education alone provides the entrée to professional success in the form of technical knowledge which is, they think, the key that unlocks all doors. This is simply not true. Nothing in life that works well is automatic, least of all strategic careering. Also, those of us who find it difficult to ask others to help us think through problems cannot, in turn, effectively help anyone else. We can't know how to help others without first getting help for ourselves. Once we experience what kinds of advice and support are truly helpful to us, we are in a better position to encourage others.

Successful people find and cultivate mentors. To Use

Catapulting well, they usually find several mentors as they progress through their various moves. They know how to apprentice themselves to older, more experienced people who, in turn, help them to present themselves more positively to different groups, position themselves more strategically in a variety of situations, and connect themselves significantly to concepts and other people *in addition to performing the technical job at hand.*

Using Catapulting is a natural process in large corporate structures. Employees have wide access to experts and potential mentors. But what about people in small businesses, or professionals in private practice? While these people have all the advantages of working for themselves, they don't have the support structure of a larger corporation. Who can their mentors be? How can they Catapult? The obvious answer lies in finding others in their fields who have made significant contributions and who are recognized for their achievement. Professional associations can provide access to such potential mentors or at least resource people. To join an association just for the opportunity to Catapult is legitimate. But you must offer your services in exchange for that opportunity. You cannot expect simply to join and have immediate results. Offer to serve on a committee or take responsibility for routine tasks. Show your interest in what is going on around you. By taking part you put yourself in the way of the people you would like to meet.

The younger you are, the more opportunities you have to use Catapulting. Colleges and graduate schools provide students with an array of faculty and administrators who can be important to them in their academic and professional careers. When I address students, I urge them to seek out those professors whose work they admire and to offer their assistance, paid or not, in research of any kind. A resulting association can be a most enriching experience and can lead to any number of new opportunities and contacts that may well be invaluable when it's time to search for a full-time position. The successful student realizes that the influence of an academic mentor is not limited to academia. Academicians have many connections to business and professional people in their own or closely related fields, connections that could be invaluable to you at the start of and throughout your career. A woman I know found her first job as a writer for a magazine through a connection provided her by one of her English professors, and there are countless others who've had similar help. Don't hesitate to ask your professors for advice about work, or for the names of any people they might know in the field you're about to enter.

Over the past several years I have been consulting with some colleges and universities to encourage development of the Critical Career Competences, especially Using Catapulting. Institutions of higher education need to train not only their students on how to approach and make use of mentors, but also their faculty on how to play their roles as mentors. Mentoring rewards a faculty member handsomely, for faculty often measure themselves—and each other—by the kinds of students they have advised and by the students' contributions to their field.

College placement services often are a graduate's first (and sometimes only) direct experience with Using Catapulting. Most college placement services have the brochures and directories of large corporations and maintain a relationship with recruiting personnel. Company representatives use the placement service to make appointments with graduating students and to publicize their entry-level and lower management positions. While this is not a substitute for making personal contacts, it is a starting place.

Let's look at the story of a twenty-year-old woman who felt completely lost. She had no family, no connections, no job, and absolutely no idea of what to do with her life. Out of desperation she went to an advertising convention in a large hotel near her apartment. She had only some slight hope that advertising was a field to which she could have access. She was too restless to sit for more than thirty minutes in the crowded conference auditorium so she just got up to wander through the exhibit hall with its many booths.

At the last booth in the middle aisle, the young woman struck up a conversation with an older, energetic woman. They talked for hours and exchanged stories about their lives. The older woman was the assistant to the president of a new, expanding advertising agency and was certainly in a position to help the younger woman, who didn't hide her admiration for her newly found mentor. On the spot, the older woman offered her a job and promised to help her along. And indeed she did. She sponsored her moves through several different departments and gave her an opportunity to learn the business. Then she encouraged her protégée to return to college and helped her decide where to go and which course of study to take. The young woman took full advantage of her mentor's advice, and seized every opportunity to learn in every position. After she graduated from college two years later, she was transferred to a branch office where she proved herself, demonstrating both talent and team sense. This year she has been transferred to New York and is enthusiastic about her future.

Sound too simple? Or like a fairy tale? Perhaps the young woman in the story was especially lucky, but her situation wasn't very different from that of many of us, nor was the outcome uncommon. But few of us have the boldness to explore. Few of us are willing to take risks or to openly admire a successful person we don't know. But if we do take some chances, we too will eventually get the support and direction we need.

# CHAPTER NINE

# Magnifying Accomplishing

*The toughest thing about success is that you've got to keep on being a success. Talent is only a starting point in this business.*

—IRVING BERLIN

*Magnifying Accomplishing* is the culmination of the six competences, a synthesis of all of the nontechnical skills introduced in these chapters. It is the natural result of successful careering and usually comes later in our careers, when we have developed our other interpersonal skills and are well on our way to reaching our goals. Then we are in a position to broaden our accomplishments, to collaborate with our colleagues, to make our expertise and experience available to others. Thus we become the mentors. In Magnifying Accomplishing we go beyond our particular job to the larger profession; we Show Belonging and Exhibit Specializing to a larger group and at a higher level. We've come a long way in our careers, have developed our abilities and our confidence to take part in an active way in many different aspects of our work. We use all of the competences in a larger context and we have become less self-conscious about using them —they have now become an integral part of our approach to work and life.

Many of the prominent lawyers I have talked with have told me about the many ways in which they magnify or broaden their areas of expertise. They serve on city and state policy committees, contribute time and money to their political party, offer their services to their bar associations, special interest groups, and humanitarian organizations. They write articles, give lectures to many of these same groups, and discuss legal matters of all kinds—pertaining to private and public concerns—with other lawyers.

I have also spoken with many scientists and artists who do similarly in the context of their professions. They participate in seminars, lecture at colleges, are active in community affairs, and speak out on social, environmental, and cultural issues. They work to find financial support for their research or to establish cultural facilities where they are needed. Successful people in every field are active in this way. Editors speak at writers' or publishers' conferences, professors read papers, visit other universities, write articles of interest to the people in their field. Doctors, businessmen, designers, publicists —all of these people bring their knowledge and experience to the largest possible audience.

We all have many opportunities to share what we know, particularly when we have refined our talents through years of experience and have grown professionally through our use of the Critical Career Competences. One of the most important and fulfilling ways to share that experience is through teaching, and we increase our own knowledge in the teaching process. Professional associations are an extremely viable arena for making our expertise and vital skills accessible to others. Let's look at how three quite different professionals Magnify their Accomplishing in their individual professions.

A prominent engineer has for many years actively participated in engineering associations. Now at the peak of her career, she has made her vast knowledge and experience available to the new generation of engineers in many ways. As board member of one association, she had been active in organizing a national engineering convention. She selected topics for discussion, invited experts of her choice to speak, designed the format for presentations. She has also served her profession by moderating and serving on expert panels, reading her research papers, and addressing the association as keynote speaker. She has published many articles in engineering and environmental journals, not only about her own scientific experiments and explorations but also about new developments for her field in general. She is a frequent contributor to her association's publication, in which she interprets the history of her field and poses questions about its future. She has taken the responsibility for educating other engineers through her commitment to her profession and her willingness to talk about her career and her work. And her gains have been considerable— in terms of her reputation as a thinking scientist and an approachable authority and in terms of her own satisfaction and fulfillment.

But don't get fooled into thinking that she or anybody like her is a born leader. This engineer is no different from the rest of us. In the beginning of her career, she was afraid to speak in public, probably the most common of all fears. But she began by speaking to small groups, quite unaware that she was just practicing in low-risk situations. Soon she was able to stop reading from her notes and found that with a minimum of preparation she could connect more readily with her audiences. She felt more free to react to people in the audience, to refer to comments of other speakers in the program, or to mention the work of a colleague if it seemed appropriate at the moment. She also became adept at collaborating with other leaders in her field who served as board members and officers. Becoming "adept" means learning how to Show Belonging while Exhibiting Specializing—working with others and being independent at the same time, until you've achieved ease in moving and doing in any situation.

The president of a public relations firm has shared his experience in the same way as the engineer. He has built his business into one of the largest and most prestigious in the country, and has participated actively in his professional associations. Like the engineer, he has acted as a mentor for many new and upwardly mobile people in his field. He has served as an officer of his association for an extended period of time, has written for journals and popular magazines, and is written about as an authority on public relations. His training of protégés is legendary, and most of them have followed him into top positions. Many come from his own company, in a pattern of moves described in the chapter on Using Catapulting; others have been drawn to him through the association. They have heard him speak and have then found an opportunity to work with him on a committee or in some other capacity.

Again, this public relations expert didn't suddenly

spring up as a great mentor, though many in his association talk about his easy wit and good fortune. From the time he was in high school, he participated in both debating and drama. He practiced early how to think about and discuss an issue, how to be "on" in public with or without stage fright, how to get along, and eventually how to win and lose, for he did both. He learned not only how to participate and how to develop a specialty but also how to lead—how to encourage others to be active and to reveal their best talents, and how to learn from both their successes and their failures. He lives and works in an intense and vital way, and his energy and commitment are examples for others.

If you were to examine the lives of successful people in any field, you would see a majority Magnifying Accomplishing by serving their professions in the ways I've described above. And their significant contributions are again magnified by those of the people they have taught and encouraged.

Another important aspect of Magnifying Accomplishing is the work that we do with our professional peers to enhance and direct our profession. We sit on boards and make financial or editorial decisions, serve on committees to allocate or find resources for new programs, or simply join together with other members of our profession to discuss our ideas, our concerns, our projects.

A highly successful lawyer serves as a perfect model for Magnifying Accomplishing. After fifteen years of exploring areas of law, he began to specialize in divorce law. After he had established himself in this field, he was invited to serve on a State Bar Association commission to draft policy for modified divorce laws. He gave a full year to the revising of the state code. Then he formed a small group of prestigious divorce lawyers who met once a month without a format. They exchanged their ideas in an informal setting and occasionally invited a judge or visiting lawyer to come and talk about his or her professional concerns.

The lawyer didn't stop at law-related activities but also became active in a large community mental-health center. He set up a series of colloquia and invited community leaders—politicians, psychiatrists, psychologists, management consultants, business executives—to discuss topics of concern with each other and with other members of the community who would make up the audience. He thereby created a forum for the exchange of ideas and an opportunity for everyone to participate in the life of the community.

Serving on bar association committees or organizing conferences requires a commitment of time and effort. It often seems futile to try to change a system, or even to bring people together to talk about the need for change, but this kind of involvement is essential to the life of any system. The people who stand out in every profession are those who use their knowledge and experience to shape their working environment on both a small and a large scale. They teach and share and encourage others to do the same; they work to enrich themselves, their professions, and their communities. They seek out opportunities to participate, to give of themselves and develop relationships with others, and they are successful because they are involved in an active and ongoing exchange with their world.

# ☐ PART III

## Introduction to the Interviews

The six Critical Career Competences comprise a hidden curriculum of successful careering. From my research and experience, successful people across every discipline demonstrate all of them. Not having labels for these competences, people act on them, consciously or not, incorporating them unnoticed into their everyday working lives.

I have interviewed four prominent people in their respective fields about their individual processes of careering. I have asked them specifically about their moves, their strategies—their Presenting, Connecting, and Positioning themselves. Instead of asking about the content of their work, I have concentrated on the context—the aspects of life and career not typically revealed. These people represent the best within a great diversity of careers and prove by their lives that these competences work.

☐ **CHAPTER TEN**

# Ely Callaway

Ely Callaway was formerly president of the textile giant, Burlington Mills. He was born into a rich American family heritage; the Callaways were founders and operators of Callaway Mills. Ely Callaway chose an independent and competitive path. Using his marketing genius, he has recently turned the California wine industry around by discovering a micro-climate for making excellent, prizewinning Callaway Wines in Southern California.

*Let's begin with early family influences in learning how to be effective. What do you recall about your parents?*

As I consider that, I realize that my mother and father had a major influence on me. I remember that my mother taught me that honesty is always the best policy. Children start out not caring whether they're honest or not. It's just not built in. We have to learn to be honest. She also taught me that the "Golden Rule" works.

*Did your father support those policies?*

Yes. And my father was the first to teach me that I could really do things if only I would just keep trying. When I would fail, he would encourage me to try again.

*Did you see him do that or did he tell you about it?*

He would tell me repeatedly, "Just keep trying; you can do it," and at the early formative stages, that had a good influence. My father was the son of a Baptist minister and very strict. In the line of major influence about how to be effective, my father's message was simply that I could achieve by continuing to try. . . . My father's influence was to make me realize that failing is not necessarily so bad. At my stage now, looking back and looking at other people, I realize that a person who is not un-

97

duly afraid of losing has taken a big step in the long process of learning how to do things successfully, because if
he fails, he's going to try again—perhaps in another direction. The fear of failure is what keeps most of us from
acting or even from making a decision. [EXPERIENCING
DOING]

*Did you go into your family's textile business?*

No. My father was with Callaway Mills, but that company had nothing at all to do with Burlington or any
other company I worked for. I never did work for the
family company. My father's older brother, Fuller Callaway, founded Callaway Mills. As it happened, Fuller
was the dominant person in that family. He would build
one company and then go on to something else, leaving
the earlier company in the hands of my father and others.

*Was there any other family member who influenced
you as a child?*

Yes, my cousin Cason Callaway, who was about
twenty-five years older than I was. Cason was a man who
was very effective with people. I remember him saying
to others when I was in my teens, "Young Ely knows
how to do things." That must have been very important
to me. At that time he was the head of Callaway Mills in
La Grange, Georgia. Besides that, he was on the board
of directors of the Shell Oil Company, the U.S. Steel
Company, and the Chemical Bank in New York. He
was a great friend of Franklin Roosevelt. In fact, when
Roosevelt would come to Warm Springs, Georgia, to swim
for his therapy, he would come over to visit at Cason's
home. Also, by his example, Cason showed me the value
of being very warm to people. He was probably the most
genial and effective man I ever knew. Most everyone
liked, admired, and respected him. His father founded
Callaway Mills and was very wealthy. As a youth, Cason
knew that he was going right on into his father's operation. He was a marvelous looking guy, with probably the
nicest smile I've ever seen on a man, besides that of my
father.

Cason also taught me that knowledge is power. He
would tell me to work hard and to learn whatever I was
supposed to learn. He emphasized that most people do
not take the trouble to work hard enough—whether it be

in studying their lessons or their competitors' companies or their own products or their competitors' products. He would say that too often we lack knowledge and therefore we lack power.

*Did you get involved in any after-school activities or jobs while you were growing up?*

I had a little route selling magazines. At that time, La Grange, Georgia, was a cotton mill town, centered around the Callaway Mills. There were only about 20,000 people working there, a small town. After school I often played basketball, and frequently earned money by selling magazines and then peaches to the neighbors. When I was ten years old, my father encouraged me to learn to play golf. [EXPERIENCING DOING]

*What made you take this job? You obviously did not have to sell magazines.*

No, I didn't have to work, and in that I was fortunate. But my father tried to influence me to do something constructive and worthwhile. He wanted me to learn things by earning a little money in order to have some independence. I remember that first job selling the *Literary Digest,* a very conservative magazine which went bust in the late Thirties. I rode my bike delivering them. But I do recall that when it was raining, my mother drove me around in her LaSalle to deliver the magazines.

*What did you do with the money you earned?*

My father advised me to make it grow. He offered one acre of our backyard, which was fairly big, for planting a certain type of peach tree which would be in some demand. I agreed and took the one hundred sixty dollars I had earned, along with money I borrowed, and bought the little peach trees. I had them planted by the yard man, pretty cheap labor, I can tell you, and the trees grew and the peaches turned out pretty good. I carted them around, selling those peaches to neighbors and some stores, earning about seven hundred dollars. I remember I enjoyed the whole thing.

*What do you remember about school itself? Did you participate in any special activity or event?*

Yes, I remember high school well. I was fairly active. I became the business manager of both the yearbook and the school newspaper. This was quite a job to get. The system was that one would be an assistant manager as a sophomore or junior and then if one sold more ads in the yearbook and the paper than anyone else, generally that person would become the business manager. That's what I did. My father encouraged me by promising me an automobile if I made it. I needed a car because selling ads took a lot of traveling. When I got the job, he presented me immediately with a secondhand Model A Ford, which was fabulous. [EXPERIENCING DOING]

*Did you play on any teams?*

Yes, a bit of basketball and baseball. But the only memorable thing I did in those days was to play golf. There was a good golf course in La Grange and I worked at it very hard. I became fairly good. Golf is a game that is unusual for several reasons. You depend only on yourself, not on a team, so you can either develop a pretty strong sense of self-confidence or you can become very, very unsure of yourself since it is an extremely difficult game. However, you can miss a shot or miss ten shots, but then pretty soon you might knock in a pretty good putt or have a few good holes so you regain your confidence. This helps to develop an attitude which is essentially one in which you're not afraid to act simply because you might fail.

Golf can also be helpful because a kid who is good enough can, at a very early age, compete with adults and win. There are very few things that a youngster can successfully do when competing against adults; a kid playing baseball, for instance, or tennis generally must play with persons his own age. But a twelve-, thirteen-, fifteen-year-old boy or girl might play far better golf than, I'd say, ninety percent of the adults. Then it is possible to get into competition with adults, the way golf tournaments are set up. As a kid playing against an adult in a golf tournament, he gets exposed to situations and problems which rarely present themselves to youngsters. I did all that. Looking back, I'd say that golf was probably the one activity which gave me the most self-confidence. Next was the selling activity for me. Selling peaches and the *Literary Digest* taught me to live with rejection. In selling you put yourself in an atmosphere of automatic rejection. The job therefore is to overcome the rejection or ignore it so that you don't personally feel rejected. [EXPERIENCING DOING]

*Did you have any sports heroes then?*

Yes, and here is a great piece of luck. It just happened that my mother was a distant cousin and friend of one of the most famous names in the sports world when I was a kid—Bobby Jones. Jones was the greatest golfer of his time, and possibly of any time to date. He lived in nearby Atlanta.

*Did you have any real relationship with him? Did he coach you or tell you stories?*

A couple of times he saw me hit the ball, and I played with him once as a child. That was very, very fortunate. He was a superb human being aside from his golf. He was a world-famous man with whom I had a modicum of a personal relationship when I was a youngster and in later life we developed a rather close friendship with each other.

*You were born into the great Callaway family. Do you think that it provided you with a special sense of connection with history? Did you feel destined or motivated or entitled?*

The whole association with the Callaway family was very helpful to me. It's nice to have your father tell you that one of your earlier ancestors, Flanders Callaway, married Daniel Boone's daghter, Jemima. Identifying even remotely with such a great historical figure must have given me some feeling of courage. Most people have no sense of connection with history at all. The blacks, for example, are tragically isolated from their history. In the Callaway family we were fortunate to have had an association with a name prominent not only in the business world but also in the religious world. There were seventeen Callaway Baptist ministers with books and newspaper articles being written about them. Callaway was a well-known name in textiles. All of this was fortunate, and I think I was able to allow this good fortune to help me rather than harm me. As you know, it's sometimes difficult for some people to accept good fortune.

*Does the Callaway Family Association meet regularly?*

Yes, and my cousin Fuller Callaway, Jr., is quite active. Some of the Callaways have developed a foundation to trace their history back as far as possible. By the way, when I first brought out our Callaway Wines in late 1975, Callaways from all over the world began to claim me as a relative—some for the first time! This was after they decided the wines were reasonably acceptable!

*How did you choose what to study and where to go to college?*

If I followed our family's expectations, I would have gone to a textile school. But even at age seventeen, I knew that I didn't particularly want to work in the family company. So I chose Emory University, a liberal arts college, rather than going to a textile engineering school. Although my father was a major factor in Callaway Mills, he did not own the company. His brother Fuller and his two nephews did. We knew that the nephews and their children would come along into the company, not me. And by that time I was developing a fairly strong sense of independence, so I really decided myself that I would go to Emory University in Atlanta.

*Were you actively involved at Emory?*

Well, I became business manager of the college yearbook, following a pattern similar to my high-school experience.

*Did you run for office of any kind?*

Yes, I was president of the senior class in 1940. [Experiencing Doing]

*Is there anything else you can recall from college?*

I had a great time, just as I did in high school. I had fun in trying to become the business manager of the high-school yearbook and the college yearbook. I made some of the honor societies, but I did not make Phi Beta Kappa which I would have liked to have done but my grades weren't good enough. I was very active in the management of my fraternity, Kappa Alpha.

*Do you still see any brothers or classmates from Emory?*
Two of my closest friends now were my classmates at Emory. One of them is James H. Wilson, of Atlanta. He is a famous lawyer, a tax expert. The other is Covington Hardee, Chairman of Lincoln Savings Bank in New York. We see each other maybe once every two or three years, but we are very close friends. Both of these outstanding lawyers went to the Harvard Law School. Wilson was number one in his class and the editor of the *Law Review*, and Hardee was number three in that same class and an associate editor of the *Harvard Law Review*. Wilson had an extremely fine record at Harvard, second only to Brandeis, and is one of the most brilliant tax lawyers in America. Prior to becoming chairman of the board of the Lincoln Savings Bank in New York, Hardee was formerly the general counsel of the Union Pacific Railroad, and also headed his own law firm in New York.

*Have you over the years talked to each other about careering choices or dilemmas?*
Yes, very often, among the three of us, and at every major junction or crisis in the respective careers of the three of us. They have been very supportive to me, and I have tried to be to them. I have lost contact with most of my other classmates.

*What did you decide to do after college graduation?*
Here's where we start to see what it's like being at the right place at the right time. I finished Emory in June of 1940. Just think of what the world was at the time. I had finished a liberal arts school where there was no ROTC. Yet within one month after I graduated I was a reserve officer, without any previous military training. Now how did that happen? Well, the only way I could get a commission so quickly after I went to Emory was through a correspondence course offered by the Quartermaster Corps. At that time the war was threatening, in some people's minds at least. Mr. Roosevelt had formed the Civilian Conservation Corps. The Army Quartermaster Corps was assigned to purchase clothing and

develop the uniforms for the CCC in 1940. So the Quartermaster and other parts of the Army were just beginning to look for reserve officers to come in and serve one year's active duty. They were beginning to recruit very aggressively in all fields. But they were just beginning; after all, Lend-Lease wasn't even approved by Congress until later. [RISKING LINKING]

*How did you know the Army needed Reserve Officers?*
The announcement was made in the newspapers, and this was pretty generally known by many. After all, a young man who felt he saw the war coming and didn't have a commission had better do something. So I read that the Quartermaster Corps was offering reserve commissions to people who would take the correspondence course. In only twenty-one days, study a few books and answer a few questions and send in the answers to the questions, and if you passed, you were a reserve officer. That's exactly what happened to me. The regulations at that time said that if you served one year's active duty you would then be relieved of your service requirement and would have your military service behind you. That sounded great to me. I was working at the Trust Company of Georgia, as a runner, meaning a messenger. I remember thinking it would be better to get my military service behind me, voluntarily, before I got started in the financial business—specifically, the factoring division of this bank in Atlanta.

So, I got my commission and signed up to serve one year's active duty at some military post anywhere. The Quartermaster asked me where I wanted to go, but I didn't know. They assumed that since I was from La Grange with the name Callaway that I would know something about the textile business. Even after I refuted that, they suggested that I serve at the Quartermaster Depot in Philadelphia, which had been the central procurement agency for all textiles and all clothing for the U.S. Army since the Revolutionary War. Three months later, in October 1940, I was stationed in Philadelphia as a second lieutenant. Pearl Harbor was December 7, 1941, fourteen months later. I didn't volunteer because I was heroic, but I felt in my own mind that we were probably going to have a war. I figured I would get my period of duty out of the way and even if I was later recalled to the Army, I would have some military experience behind me. At any rate, I went in with the basic idea of getting my military service behind me and then going back to work at the bank. I was given an assignment in the procurement department and became an assistant contracting officer, which means an assistant buyer. All this detail is important to my life. The Quartermaster Corps assigns certain men to be known as contracting officers. These officers are appointed special agents of the government to make contracts on behalf of the United States Government and to administer those contracts to be sure that the Army obtains what it needs. I was only twenty-two years old, knowing very little, and barely of legal age to sign a contract when I was given that responsibility.

A year later I was appointed as a full contracting officer. I was also appointed assistant to Colonel Thomas Jones, who just happened to be from Atlanta, Georgia. He was a marvelous young regular Army officer who took me under his wing. He was genial and warm and soft even though he was a professional Army man. And, he was the senior officer in charge of buying all the textiles and apparel for the entire Army, a relatively small organization at that time.

Within one year, my year of active duty was up. I could be relieved of duty or I could remain. So I decided to remain. This was now October of 1941 and I felt strongly we were going to have a war with Germany, not Japan. I felt that if I left the Army I'd only be called back soon. So I stayed at Philadelphia.

*Did the colonel help you make that decision?*

Although he wouldn't make the decision for me, he did point out that he wanted me to continue as his assistant, and that we'd be in a pretty good spot. Pearl Harbor came only two months later. Within one year we had five thousand civilian employees at the Philadelphia Quartermaster Depot—spending at the rate of two billion dollars a year on textiles and clothing. We were, in short, practically running the entire textile and apparel industries of the United States. As the war developed and the clothing requirements increased tremendously for an army of ten million men, this was one of the most active business/military operations in history. I remained in that assignment for the next four years and advanced to the rank of major by the time I was twenty-four.

*Were you going out to deal with the apparel industry?*
Yes. When the Army wants a shirt, first the Army buys the cotton fabric because the fabric has to meet certain specifications. When the fabric is on hand or in depots all over the world, then the Army orders the manufacture of the shirts—to be made from the Army's fabric. That's where my job would begin. Taking the procurement directive, I'd go to the entire cotton apparel industry in America and send them official invitations to bid within a specific time. Often we would be offered only one-half of what we had asked for because the industry didn't want to give up all of its productive capacity to the military. My job as a contracting officer was to get on the telephone all day long from about eight in the morning until eight at night. I'd call up the head of the company and beg him to give us twice as much of his production as he wanted to. That's all I did. I worked at that pace constantly every day for about four years. We bought about seventy-five percent of the entire production of the entire cotton garment industry's productive capacity for four and a half years without ever having to give out one mandatory order. That was a selling job. [Risking Linking]

*Try to recall how you were able to persuade these presidents or officers to produce at a greater rate for the military without federal mandate.*
Let me give you a specific example of trying to buy the production of, let's say, five million fatigue suits. I'd send out an invitation to bid, that is, a formal, written specification, to that portion of the cotton apparel industry we knew could produce this item. They would send back their bids and we would open and analyze them. In total, they might offer to produce only three million units, making us short two million. My staff would then prepare abstracts, huge sheets of paper with the pertinent details of every bid, listing the manufacturer, how much he offered, at what price, delivery schedule, etc. In a short time, I would determine manufacturer's productive capacity. I also had the information validated by inspectors who were stationed at the bidders' plants.

So, for example, I would notice that Carroll Rosenbloom (then head of Blue Ridge Manufacturing Company in Huntington, West Virginia) had not offered as much as we felt he could produce for us. There would be many other firms which we knew could offer to produce larger quantities. So it went, all across the board. I assigned some assistants to call up the major manufacturers and try to get them to increase their offerings by various amounts. We asked the manufacturers to reconsider and respond by telegram. Even after that we might still be short one million units. If so, I would then personally telephone the head of various companies or his main assistant and would try to persuade him to offer greater quantities. My request had to be realistic. [EXHIBITING SPECIALIZING]

*What takes so much time when you are representing the government at war?*

Well, we had to learn all about the manufacturer's productive capacity before we could realistically determine how much he could do for us. After some experience, the manufacturers knew I was fair, not requesting any single manufacturer to do more than his fair share. This is a matter of honesty and treating people equitably. I never tried to force any one manufacturer to devote all of his production to the Army. I found that generally when the manufacturer discovered that he was in good hands, not in the hands of an unreasonable Army man, he would respond generously. And, of course, we appealed to their patriotism. [SHOWING BELONGING]

*What constitutes building a relationship over a year? What did you actually do?*

You become valuable to the person, by acting in such a way that he will trust, respect, and, hopefully, like you. I developed a very close relationship with many of our suppliers to the Army in the work clothing business. We spoke to each other three or four times a week over a period of three or four years. Carroll Rosenbloom, the late owner of the Los Angeles Rams, was a good example. In those days Carroll ran a very large and successful work clothing manufacturing company. He was patriotic and very helpful to the Army. Now here was a man who learned how to be very successful at doing a wide variety of things. Carroll branched out into fields that were totally unrelated, and became extremely successful. He was very wealthy and was one of the great personalities of the football world. I recall that he was a close personal friend of Jack Kennedy's before and during his presidency.

*Did you get any kind of special recognition for this kind of production-getting?*

I sure did. I was made a major when I was twenty-four years old, which was about as good a recognition as I wanted and fantastic for those days. I was the youngest major among two million men in the Quartermaster Corps. I was sitting at a desk, totally protected, yet I exposed myself from the minute I went into the Army in 1940 to being called anywhere at any time. I stayed in that job five years and I had only one move, one transfer from Philadelphia to New York to go with Colonel Jones. My military experience was something of great benefit to me while most people were being shot at and killed. I was very lucky.

*Let's look at the luck factor more closely. Compare yourself with the other contracting officers. Did you produce more contracts than they? What if you hadn't been productive in your assignment?*

I would have been shipped out. There's no doubt about it. In fact, some of the twenty-five I originally entered the Army with were called back, but they all lost their seniority in the job. By remaining at Philadelphia, I put myself in the position of being offered the job as official contracting officer in 1942.

*So now when the war was over, you were connected to all the presidents of all the big apparel companies?*

Yes, that's correct, and all the textile people knew me by then because I had been at Philadelphia so long in a senior position. I received many job offers from the apparel manufacturing companies, but I wanted to go into the textile business. I went to see my father, who was very close to me at that point. He was proud of me for having held a job with important responsibility and for having moved up fairly well in the ranks on my own. He helped me decide which of the textile companies to choose from, weighing the best prospect, their financial resources, their prospects, etc. I was offered several top positions among the textile mills. At that time, I was twenty-six years old. [RISKING LINKING]

I chose to work for Roger Milliken of Deering, Milliken & Company, Inc., a very large progressive and privately owned company. I knew that if I ended up at the top of the textile business I'd have to be in New York, the merchandising headquarters for the textile world. However, I wanted to spend a few years in Atlanta learning the textile business and selling textiles in the southeast to the apparel manufacturers with whom I had dealt during the war. I proposed to Roger that I establish a southeastern sales office, stay there for only a few years and then I'd go anywhere. Milliken agreed. Three years later, after doing a pretty good job of selling Milliken textiles all over the southeast, traveling an awful lot, Roger proposed that I move to New York and head up a new division. He had just constructed several new woolen and worsted mills. He wanted me to set up a men's-wear business and make worsted fabrics to sell to the men's-wear trade. So I did that. [USING CATAPULTING]

*How did you go about knowing what to do to start?*

I had to learn the tailored clothing trade—Hart Schaffner & Marx, and people of that kind, because I had been dealing previously with work-clothing manufacturers. I found out who the best worsted salesmen were, the best fabric stylist, colorist, then I went out and hired them to join this new division of Milliken. I built up that division, which became quite famous after we developed some terrific new fabrics, developing the newest synthetic fibers blended with high-price fine wool. We created the first dacron and wool fabrics in the United States, and we sold them. They were fabrics every bit as fine as traditional wool fabrics from England and yet with a performance characteristic that was unique and better for the consumer. The fabrics held a crease in the rain! And they were much more resistant to wrinkling than anything developed previously.

We worked closely with DuPont in developing these new fabrics. All the chemical companies who were making fibers would come to the textile mills with their new products. We would listen to them, being more receptive to these new ideas than most of our competitors were. We developed several new fabrics that were really successful. My department grew very big. In 1954 I left Milliken. [RISKING LINKING]

*Why? Did you get a better offer?*
No, I was fired.

*Why were you fired?*
I'm sure that anyone who gets fired never knows all the reasons why. But I think the main reason in my case was that my boss at Milliken was the owner's brother-in-law. He was a very bright young fellow, but we argued all the time. I think he finally got tired of arguing with me, so he fired me. Looking back, I don't blame him.

*Were you married? Did you have children at this time?*
Yes, and I was pretty upset for a few days. Then I began to get such terrific offers that my ego became unwounded. I began to feel even better than ever.

*How did people know that you were fired?*
The news of my "resignation" was on the front page of the trade papers.

*What was your title at that time?*
I was the general manager in charge of the men's-wear division of Deering, Milliken. I was thirty-five years old and making one of the highest salaries in the textile industry—for my age.

*To reach this key position, tell me what you actually did for the company in addition to hiring the best people you could find, and using new technologies from Du-Pont.*
We substantially increased the profitability of the company. As head of the department, I encouraged the development of new and better fabrics and then I went to the market to help sell them—at relatively high prices. This was a tough selling job, because the traditional clothing manufacturer in the early 1950's did not want to become involved with a synthetic product. It initially

seemed like a cheapening influence, yet we were charging more for the product. [Exhibiting Specializing]

Generally, to be successful in any business, one has to create a new and better product or service and then understand how to articulate the benefits of that product to the consumer or buyer in an intelligent, persuasive way. Business success usually calls for creative merchandising. That is an ability to create something for somebody that they want, but which they don't know they want until it is brought to their attention and demonstrated. That's what we did later with nylon panty hose, for instance. American women did not even conceive of the benefits of panty hose before they were created. However, we knew that if such a product were developed and offered to them, American women would buy a product which would bring them added comfort, convenience, and better appearance. So the successful merchant is one who understands these desires or those unexpressed, unarticulated wants, puts them into a new and better product and thus creates a new need.

*At the same time, were you in contact with your counterparts in other companies?*

Yes, but our antitrust laws did, and still do, limit one's involvement with one's competitors. I was very careful along these lines to stay within the law.

*Did you do any speaking or writing?*

Yes, quite frequently. [Magnifying Accomplishing]

*What happened to you after you were fired from Milliken?*

I had heard about a big event then going on in the textile world. Royal Little was the first creator of the true conglomerate in America. He was the genius behind a company called Textron in Rhode Island, and was forming a merger of several different textile operations, including the American Woolen Company, a great old industrial giant of New England. That company had nothing but cash, but was going downhill. Little merged American Woolen with two or three other textile companies and hired Bob Huffines, the ex-president of Burlington, to put together the merger. It was an exciting development and Huffines offered me the job of taking over this big woolen and worsted operation which was part of the merger. I had numerous other offers from much safer companies, but this one was an interesting gamble. I joined Textron and eighteen months later Royal Little sold Burlington Industries the division that I was running. I went with the sale or the acquisition. [RISKING LINKING]

*Did you weigh the risks or the gamble? Did you consider failure?*

Sure, but I figured the positive chances outweighed the negative. So I decided to go. I certainly never wanted to be fired from Milliken; that seemed to be a real failure at the time. But, I was willing to take a risk again and so I moved to Textron.

*Did you make any attempt to talk to the brother-in-law who was your boss after you were fired by him?*

No, I knew that Roger Milliken would support him, so I just left. In my new position at Textron we had to build a new organization of experienced men in the woolen and worsted field, so in selecting the key men for my new organization, I turned to the men I knew best. Within six months after leaving Milliken, I hired four key men from the worsted division of Milliken, and brought them into key positions at Textron. Two months after that, Roger Milliken fired his brother-in-law, my former boss who had discharged me.

*Where did you go then?*

About eighteen months after I joined Textron, the greatest individual in the textile industry came along—Spencer Love. Spencer Love founded Burlington Industries from nothing in 1923 and at his death in 1962, about forty years later, Burlington was the giant of the whole textile world. Love wasn't a wealthy man; he was the son of a professor at Harvard. He had been through World War I and came out as the youngest infantry captain in World War I. In 1923 he heard about a small bedspread manufacturer in Burlington, North Carolina, when rayon was in its infancy. He saw a good new product, and he was determined to get in the business. He courageously borrowed most of the money for that operation and he then began, over the first fifteen or twenty years of Burlington's existence, borrowing money very heavily, always on the border of going out of business, just barely making it. But Spencer Love and his new company, Burlington, survived because he knew he could, no matter what were the odds against him. [USING CATAPULTING]

In 1956, Love purchased from Royal Little the division of Textron which I was running, and thus I became a part of Burlington Industries. Love had already purchased Pacific Mills, an old New England woolen and worsted operation, doing $150 million, second to American Woolen Company. I started out as a vice-president of this new division of Burlington and then I moved up to a vice-presidency and then presidency of Pacific Mills in two years. Three years later, I got involved in the Burlington parent company, first as a senior officer, then as president.

*In those early five years, what do you think you did that made you visibly valuable?*

The division that I was running was extremely profitable, while the similar one that Burlington owned, Pacific Mills, was not profitable. I selected strong, able men for my division, and we set about creating new and better products. We were successful at merchandising, and soon moved into the ranks of the most profitable divisions of our new parent, Burlington Industries. [EXHIBITING SPECIALIZING]

*What happened while you were president of Pacific?*

Spencer Love, Burlington's chief executive, soon asked me to help him run other divisions of Burlington, at the same time retaining the responsibility for the ones I had helped to build. Love put me on the senior management committee and then made me a corporate officer of the parent company. We had a close personal as well as a sound working relationship. Spencer Love was one of the industrial geniuses of this country. He was also an extremely difficult and complex man—probably one of the most difficult industrialists to relate to. He liked the idea, for instance, of playing one top man against another within Burlington. This made survival difficult for at least half of his top managers.

*What made you survive?*

It was essentially the continuing profitability of the divisions for which I was responsible. If we hadn't been profitable I would have been out just like any other. Love was impressed by the results. He felt that I had courage, vision, a pretty good understanding of people, and an ability to encourage and develop strong men within my divisions. I think that's the answer he would have given you had you asked him this question. While many of Love's division heads were afraid to hire strong men, I wasn't. I began to attract people from within the company and from all over the industry. I had a record of hiring and developing very strong, able people, giving them a lot of authority and responsibility, not getting in their way, and paying them a lot of money if they did well.

*Let me ask about the Burlington Mills Exhibit at its New York headquarters on Sixth Avenue in New York— known as "The Mill." It is to me a symbol of New York, a synthesis of industry and art. Did you have anything to do with it?*

Yes, I did—quite directly, too. There are very few successful industrial exhibits in New York City and the ones that I have seen are generally pretty dull. They're usually not hit shows. But I thought that Burlington could develop one. If you have a theater in the big city, located well, then the only thing that you need to do is have a hit show to attract a big audience. Burlington had the theater; our office was in America's largest city, located next to the Hilton Hotel with a million visitors per year directly next to us. [EXHIBITING SPECIALIZING]

I wanted a hit show and knew we would have to spend around a million and a half dollars to produce it. For approval of this amount of money, I had to go to the Board of Directors with the concept and convince them it would be a sound move. Even though I was president of Burlington, many of our directors were cold on the idea. My belief was that people are very interested in learning about the manufacturing processes involved in producing a product which they can relate personally to. We know that people are moved by color, sound, action. We wanted to put all of those things together to duplicate the interest and excitement of walking through a textile mill. When you walk through a textile mill, you get really excited; there's a lot of sound and movement, intricate machinery banging away, colors and steam and everything. I felt that if we could capture that and transfer it into this great theater in our office on Sixth Avenue, we would attract the attention and interest of a great many people valuable to Burlington. They tell me it has worked. I understand that "The Mill" has attracted more than four million visitors.

*How about the awards you've won—Boy Scouts, National Conference of Christians and Jews, and positions as trustee on boards?*

Some of the awards came mainly because of my position as president of Burlington. But as a personal choice, I headed the National Corporate Donations Committee for United Negro College Fund. I have long wanted to help the black people and have also been a strong supporter of Jewish causes throughout my career. I was always supportive of the blacks, even though I came from Georgia. Growing up in Georgia, I saw blacks deprived of education and equal rights under the law—just as simple and tragic as that. [MAGNIFYING ACCOMPLISHING]

I have been very interested in the whole problem of emotional health of people, in general and specifically. I was very close to Dr. Will Menninger, who ran Menninger with his brother, Dr. Karl. Dr. Will asked me to come on his board before I was president of Burlington. I had a lot of exposure to emotional problems among people very close to me—my older sister and others. I witnessed much suffering among friends and loved ones. So, I began to help raise money for the Menninger Foundation in Topeka, Kansas. Today, I am still doing this and am personally close to Dr. Roy Menninger, head of the Menninger complex.

*Let me ask you about openly competing with your family's business, or were you able to help Callaway Mills during that time in the Army or afterward?*

We were always competitors. Callaway was making fabrics and I was competing with them. At Milliken and Burlington, we were direct competitors, making the same kinds of fabrics, selling to the same customers.

*Did your father's nephew Cason ever extend an offer to you?*

No, but shortly before Cason Callaway died, Spencer

Love and I were talking to him about buying Callaway Mills. Cason was all for it, but it ended up that his brother, Fuller Jr., who was then in active control of Callaway Mills, sold that company to Roger Milliken.

In my opinion, this was the best move for Fuller Callaway to make. It met his needs perfectly and was good for Milliken. But it's interesting to speculate or contemplate that perhaps if Callaway Mills had been sold to Burlington, at that time, the Ely Callaway "circle" would have, in one sense, been completed.

*How did you make contributions to the textile field? I know you said you're in competition with others in the field, but did you also take steps together with them?*

Yes, competitors sometimes work together against a common enemy, for a common cause. In the case of the textile business, the common enemy is imports from abroad made with cheap labor and dumped in the U.S. market below cost. You have to cope with that enemy together and you ask for "protection" through and by the U.S. government. The industry approaches the federal government and asks for legal protection against unfair competition from abroad. Suddenly the businessman, who usually wants to get rid of the government, now asks for a favor from that same government.

*Did you go the the government yourself or were you representing the textile association?*

Primarily through the textile associations. Occasionally, I was very active in that group and once went at their request to a Senate subcommittee on international trade. *The New York Times* knew that I was an unofficial spokesman and wrote an article based on my testimony in 1971. [Risking Linking]

*Did you hold any elected office in the trade association?*

I did not personally, but Burlington's chairman was president of the association. That was enough for our company to do. I have always been very much an individual in voicing my views on how the government should help the industry.

*How have you supported or encouraged people to thrive in any one or more of the divisions of Burlington, in addition to making profits?*

I encouraged and supported people by enabling them to develop their personal potentials to the fullest. I encouraged them to take additional responsibilities, and to take reasonable risks; I gave them authority to act, reasonable backing when they made mistakes, and encouragement to try again—up to a point.

*Did you single out people to bring along? What did you look for in picking them originally?*
Yes, I did—very frequently. I looked for honesty and integrity; emotional stability; dedication; knowledge of the job; vision and imagination; decisiveness and courage; effectiveness with people.

*How did you know or find that out?*
Mainly by observing them on a close personal basis; by noticing and judging their job performance; by talking to their customers and company associates about these individuals; by talking with members of their families (wives and husbands); and by talking with our competitors about these persons and their abilities and personal characteristics.

*Let's look at such modeling in your personal life with your children. Your father encouraged you to work. Did you similarly encourage your children to work too?*
I encouraged them to be self-reliant. There were two points that I insisted on. I gave them the best education wherever they wanted to pursue it. I also wanted them to be independent, not looking to go in business with me. I wanted to help prepare them to be on their own. I tended to push them out of the nest, but let them know they could always return.

*Did you help them with actual school work?*
No, not much of that. They didn't need it. Although I hope I've been a good model to them, I never emphasized the need to go out and sell newspapers or peaches. I think their mother did; she was concerned with their being frugal, not throwing money away. I expect too that at the time these kids were growing up I never realized how my early work habits had influenced me. If I had, I might have gone the other way. But it turns out that none of my children were interested in business until they be-

came adults. Perhaps the times were very different. The attitude of a young person toward business in the late Fifties and the Sixties was totally different than when I grew up. Businessmen were heroes to my generation; they were villains to my children's generation. Now they have all come around, I'm happy to say.

*What do you think about people moving up in the business world to enhance their own careers by stepping on others?*

I'm sure a lot of that happens, but in my experience it doesn't have to be that way. I know I never did it and I saw so many who were able, lucky, performing well and relating very successfully to all types of people without being inconsiderate, superaggressive, or mean. But, I have also seen some "successful" businessmen who were downright dishonest, totally self-centered, and rather severely neurotic in some important areas of their selves. Fortunately, such types are in the minority, and are passing from the scene.

*When you say "lucky," what do you mean?*

For one thing, being "lucky" can often mean simply the absence of a lot of bad luck in one's life. Furthermore, it depends on whether you're talking about a business career, or personal health. In a business career "luck" can mean being at the right place at the right time, with the right people, with the right amount of knowledge to seize an opportunity that comes up. One thing I find most interesting in business is that nearly everything one does in solving a business problem has to do with people. Able people working in reasonable harmony to accomplish a joint goal together is one of the most difficult things to achieve in business. The most successful businesses generally are the ones which are able to develop such teamwork. Most job failures I observed have been failures due to one's inability to work in reasonable harmony with one's associates toward a common goal.

*What do you see that holds most people back?*

Very often people who don't know what to do about their careers are in that dilemma because they don't know how to make a decision. Their inability to make a decision is based on their fear of losing—of making the wrong decision. Therefore they don't decide to go ahead and do something. They are unable to take a direction and follow it. I think that's the main problem with those who never utilize their talents and never get anywhere; they don't make the first courageous decision to act and to continue to act. That is a very sad waste of talent and waste of energy. Learning to cope with the fear of losing is very important. All of us have a fear of losing to a certain extent. The most effective people are certainly not always fearless.

But successful action comes from the ability to control, ignore, or cope with normal fears. And very often knowledge is the power that dissolves fears. The successful ones are those who will act without being unduly inhibited by fear. Such people free up their talents and creative energies and motivate others to do the same thing. A leader of any department in a company, or of a nation, must take decisive and courageous action. One should set the pace and prove by example that one can take the risks and try again if success is not achieved at first. It is most important to know that we learn to be successful by doing. [EXPERIENCING DOING]

*What did you choose to do after Burlington?*
I decided to produce wine in Southern California. In 1969, three years before I left Burlington, I planted my vineyard and thus took the first major step toward entering the wine business. [EXPERIENCING DOING]

*What did you know about making wine?*
I didn't know anything, but I knew that the wine business was probably going to be a good bet in this country. Therefore, in 1974, a year after I left Burlington, I constructed a winery and hired experts to help me enter the wine business. Without sounding too boastful, I'd say this was my best vision. I'll never have a better vision. In 1969 I knew I could start growing wine grapes and that if I ever retired from Burlington I could come to Temecula and build a winery on my vineyard. I retired a bit sooner than I expected though. I was ready to move on. I always worked very hard and I was always in love with my job like I am right now. I'm returning to being a farmer. I always wanted to end up as I started —with a peach orchard, farming. Now I am farming,

converting my farm product to another product—wine
—and am controlling the merchandising of the finished
item. One can't do that if one grows cotton or lettuce,
oranges, peaches, potatoes, etc. If one wants to completely control the merchandising of one's farm product
direct to the consumer, one almost has to be in the wine
business. So it was a merchandising decision that made
me get into the wine business. Almost everything I have
ever done in business has had a merchandising orientation behind it. So much of life involves merchandising—
selling an idea, a service, or a product. [RISKING LINK-
ING]

*You did the same thing here that you did every other
place, that is, you found the best experts to give you the
best advice.*
That's right. No other way makes sense to me.

*How did you convince wine buyers to buy your high-
priced wine grown in Southern California when everyone
knows that the best comes from Northern California?*
It was the toughest selling job I've ever had, including
those magazines in La Grange. Wine, by its nature, is a
product that is sold largely on image. The sales appeal
of wine is usually determined largely by the history of the
vineyard, where it was located—in Bordeaux, Médoc, the
Rhineland or Napa Valley. The location of the vineyard
and the experience and background of the family producing it are a large part of the appeal of high-priced wine.
In the case of Callaway Vineyard and Winery, in the
early days of selling our wines we had a negative image
and no history.

We first went out with our line in the fall of 1975 when
the wine market had taken a nose dive. We had a combination of nothing but negative factors. The only plus
was the quality of the wine in the bottle. So we had a
unique combination of many barriers to overcome in the
world of merchandising. It certainly was the toughest I'd
ever seen. [RISKING LINKING]
But my sales manager, Ed Russell, and I persuaded
some key retailers, restaurants, and wine writers to try
the wines. Many of them were very favorably impressed;
they endorsed our wines publicly; these influential people
talked or wrote about our wines; this influenced others;

and simply by hard work, we knocked on many doors and many of them opened up to us. [EXHIBITING SPECIALIZING]

*You must have had some network to help you. Did you know any of the wine critics like Robert Balzer who have built their reputations as wine experts?*
I met none of these people until after I had completed the winery and had almost finished the processing of our first vintage. I am referring to wine writers, wine retailers, and restaurant owners in California. In 1973 and 1974, I was fortunate to meet Leon Adams, Professor Harold Berg of the U.C. Davis, and Andre Tchelistcheff. Each of these men gave me technical advice and counsel, but not about selling.

*Wasn't the wine trade curious about where you had come from and who you were?*
Yes, they were. Because we were trying to do something the experts considered unwise or impossible, we naturally attracted attention. I expected that if the wines were received favorably, they would quickly create special attention and comments. [EXHIBITING SPECIALIZING]

*How long after you produced your first wines did you get publicity?*
We crushed the first white grapes in September and October, 1974, and began to sell the resulting wines one year later. I didn't want to go out and try to get a good press before the wines were ready to sell.

About two months before we went to the general market, I invited Robert Balzer to come to the winery and taste the wines. He was the first and only wine writer we allowed to taste the wines at that time. Fortunately, he was favorably impressed, and he so advised his readers. After that we received mostly favorable comment from the critics, and some unfavorable. A few of these professionals are still irritated with us—some of them because we dared to make our moves without first consulting them; some because they simply don't want to reverse their long-held statements that fine wines cannot come from Southern California; some do not like the taste of our style of wine; and a couple of them are irritated that I refuse to pay for their attentions.

The greatest amount of publicity came to us immediately afterward; our 1974 White Riesling was the only wine served to Queen Elizabeth II at a bicentennial luncheon for seventeen hundred people given in honor of Her Majesty and Prince Philip at the Waldorf in New York, July 9, 1976. Prior to that time, we were almost unknown outside California, and very new to the California wine scene. The fact that a Callaway wine was chosen for that major event caused many people to credit the choice to our blind luck, or to my special influence with those who chose our wine for that luncheon, or they claimed that I gave all the wine to the sponsoring committee—*gratis,* or that I had some special influence with the White House (which had nothing at all to do with the New York luncheon). A few persons unduly flattered me by saying that I even had some kind of mysterious influence with the Queen! That luncheon was sponsored by The Pilgrims Society of N.Y., and the English Speaking Union of New York.

Well, the truth is that the wine was chosen for that occasion simply because the sponsoring organization's food and wine committee tasted many wines and decided that ours was the one that most successfully complemented the flavors of the foods on the menu that they had chosen to serve to the Queen. Before they made that choice, I did not know any of the wine committee members, nor did I ever ask anyone to submit my wine for consideration. But, the fact that we were new, unknown, and from Southern California did create a special interest and, therefore, the resulting publicity was, fortunately for us, quite extensive. We still hear about it nearly every day.

*Initially did you have your greatest sales success in Southern California or elsewhere?*

During the summer of 1975, I tried to sell to a few wine retailers in Southern California, one or two in Beverly Hills, Orange County, San Diego, and got pretty much a negative reaction. So I decided we should take another approach. And that was to go to New York to a few prestigious customers who would influence the Californians if the New Yorkers would buy. And they did. I persuaded two or three of the best wine stores and restaurants there, like the Four Seasons, to purchase the wines and to endorse them to the trade—in other words to put their opinions on paper and to allow me to reprint their letters of endorsement. [EXHIBITING SPECIALIZING]

*Did you know these New York buyers previously?*

I knew only Paul Kovi of the Four Seasons—one out of the three I first sold. For instance, until I walked into his office, sat down with him, and practically forced him to taste the wine, I had never seen Sam Aaron, head of the prestigious store, Sherry-Lehmann. Sam liked what he tasted and agreed to buy almost immediately. I asked him and Peter Morrell, another prestigious retailer, to write me a letter giving their reaction to the wines and I asked them to let me take their letters and do whatever I wanted to with them. They were willing, and so were Paul Kovi and a couple of others. Armed with this, I returned to California and approached several of the leading merchants in San Francisco and one leading retailer in the Napa Valley. Each of these leaders in Northern California responded favorably, and then I found it easier to sell to the customers I wanted in Southern California and later in other states. These initial sales efforts took me about three months. After that, I hired Ed Russell to head up our merchandising and he was very effective.

*What was your advertising plan?*

We have not spent any money on advertising space—oh, well, maybe three hundred dollars total in the past three years. I do believe in advertising, but since we are small and received a lot of publicity, we have had no need to advertise in the normal sense.

*Do you want the Callaway Winery to become much larger?*

No. We are already California's second or third largest winery in our price and quality category. I think that we are probably second in size—behind only Sterling Winery, now owned by Coca-Cola of Atlanta. With my limited funds, we can't possibly catch Sterling and don't need to. We can be very profitable at our current size.

We've already achieved our number-one goal, which

was to make a wine that was impressive enough to make Southern Californians proud of it. That's why we have tripled in size since we built the winery in 1974. We have grown because the wines are pleasing to many people, and we are the only producer of our type wines in Southern California—a huge market for the higher-priced wines. In other words, we have discovered our particular niche in the market—our reason for being. Our product itself and the location of our winery in relation to the Southern California market makes us of special value to our customers in this most exciting growth area of the United States. For success in any business, it's important that the company develop a unique or special value for the market it intends to supply. You'd be surprised at how rarely this is done. We now have an edge because the negatives we had in the beginning have now been turned into pluses. Now there are no negatives to the Callaway label, or to the location of our vineyard and winery. And, our wines sell very well in many of the finer restaurants in San Francisco. We are oriented toward supplying the restaurant trade—our wines go well with a wide variety of foods, and we do our best to give our restaurants a continuous supply—something that is extremely difficult to do. [EXHIBITING SPECIALIZING]

*Have you had any direct influence on the wine industry in these few years?*

Well, I expect that many in the industry don't know we exist. Perhaps the only influence we may have had on some is to encourage them to consider the soils and the micro-climatic factors which exist at any given exact spot in California when considering where to plant a vineyard —rather than consider the large, regional guidance previously recommended by most experts.

Some of our winemaking procedures are quite different from others in California, but I doubt that our competitors take any notice.

Most of the people in the wine business don't understand why we get so much publicity. They think it's because I have a merchandising background and money enough to buy the publicity. They don't believe we have adopted a simple concept—i.e., making a good wine under conditions considered impossible in the middle of the biggest wine market in the world just about guarantees a tremendous amount of free publicity.

*How do you manage favors to old business friends and new ones?*

First, let me tell you about pricing. We studied our competitors' wines from Northern California and priced our wines at the same levels as those of comparable quality. I also have a policy and a practice of giving all customers the opportunity to buy our wines at the same price his competitor pays for our wine. In other words, we give everyone the opportunity to buy at the same price. We play no favorites. We do offer standard quantity discounts, but every customer is aware of the discounts and each can utilize them if they want. I follow this practice because, first, it's right; and second, it's legal. I learned this principle in the Army; it became known that I didn't give anyone special benefits or treatment. This is where my ethical training at home from my mother and father could be illustrated. Furthermore, I have learned throughout my career that fair treatment pays off eventually.

*What is your personal future with the winery?*

Well, apparently no one's ready to fire me yet. I want to be active in management and have at least some substantial ownership in the company for a long time.

I can visualize taking in a financial investor at some point a few years hence. None of my children are interested in coming into the wine business as a career. If one wanted to and had the financial means, this company could be developed into being a very large factor in the California wine business some day. I have neither the desire nor the financial resources to do that. We figure that just to duplicate the relatively small vineyard and winery we have today would require an investment of about ten million dollars and, of course, ten years if one started today.

*What's on the horizon after your success with the winery?*

I'm probably going to start a new business. If we do, that new company will bottle and sell drinking water in Southern California.

*Was this planned all along?*

No, it wasn't. We very recently discovered that a 1,000-foot-deep well underneath the Callaway vineyard provides a very large supply of clean, good-tasting mineral water. These two businesses tie together in a sense. Just as it was a sound concept for me to go into higher-priced wine production in Southern California, it makes sense for me to seriously consider bottling the mineral water that comes from this deep well underneath my vineyard. It makes sense because this good-tasting mineral water is so clean it does not have to be chlorinated, and the source of the water is in the middle of America's largest market for bottled water. We will have to transport the Callaway Deep Well Mineral Water not more than one hundred twenty-five miles to this huge market —rather than move it five thousand miles as Perrier does. In all of Southern California, there is no major source of mineral water from a very deep well, as far as I know.

At least thirty percent of all of the bottled water sold in the U.S. in 1978 was consumed in Southern California —within a maximum of a hundred twenty-five miles from this water source underneath the Callaway vineyard.

*How did you discover this water? Is this a case of opportunity coming in clearly labeled bottles?*

It was partly accidental. One hot August 1978 day when I was out in the vineyard by the well, I noticed a faucet and wondered what the water would taste like. So I turned it on, let it run awhile, and drank it out of my hands. It tasted very good. I decided to have the water analyzed immediately by a laboratory and went back to the well by myself and filled up a couple of bottles without telling anybody. At the same time, I bought some Perrier and other waters and had them all analyzed along with mine in a laboratory in Riverside for a cost of four hundred dollars. In the meantime, I kept drinking it and offered it casually to other people, without telling them what it was. Everyone agreed it was good-tasting water. When the lab analysis was completed, it was very encouraging. Incidentally, this deep well was dug and completed before I planted the vineyard. But I had never bothered to check to see how the water tasted. To date this well water has been used to irrigate our vineyard. [RISKING LINKING]

*Why didn't you tell anybody?*

I think that one should not talk about a new product until one knows a lot about the product and has a definite plan for merchandising and delivering it.

*What will you do with it? Do you own the water rights?*

I made a presentation to the Board of Directors of the Rancho California Water District, and they will give me their reply soon. We know we can buy the water; we're doing that now. But what I want to do is to assure the supply from that particular well. My guess is that the Water District will make an agreement with us. I suggested to these Water District officials that I will bottle this water and sell it locally. Our local citizens are not happy with our local tap water because of the need for chlorination. I told them that I will set up a new company and will share the success of the company with the Water District. I'll give something for something. I will give them an opportunity to get good-tasting water locally and then will try to sell this water in bottles throughout Southern California—thus helping to publicize Rancho California and Temecula as well as providing some added income for the Water District, if my idea is successful.

*How have you contributed to Temecula?*

We are a major employer in the local community and have made one of the largest investments in this community. This can mean continuous employment. We also attract a lot of visitors and this generates local business and helps to create interest in the whole area, a ninety-thousand-acre real estate development owned by Kaiser. Rancho California was originally owned by a partnership, Kaiser and Aetna Insurance Company. Aetna Insurance Company in Hartford, Connecticut, saw that my winery could be valuable to them and they have become a major lender to my company. They have since split with Kaiser.

*What are some of the major factors that make for success in business?*

One of the most important factors is that the business must be soundly conceived. There must be a special reason for the existence of the company's product or service. Too many people go into business simply because they think they are able and smart and are blessed with transferable skills. Secondly, you must be able to make your product better or cheaper than your competitors' and/or bring new features to it that will be appreciated and wanted. Certainly, a successful company must be blessed with excellent management and have adequate financing. The latter is becoming daily more of a problem for the small entrepreneur in America. Wall Street has practically dried up as a source of venture capital. The big banks generally are so conservative they won't lend a developing, young American company any money unless the company is so well financed that the credit isn't really necessary. What this condition does is to greatly inhibit the creation of small venturesome companies and it forces the big, wealthy companies to become bigger and wealthier.

But, probably the single most important factor behind any successful business is the belief in the objectives and the potential of the company and its products on the part of the owner and the chief executive officer and all of their associates. That's my opinion, anyway.

# CHAPTER ELEVEN

# Dom DeLuise

Dom DeLuise is a native of Brooklyn, New York, and a graduate of the High School of the Performing Arts. He had a love for acting as a young child and landed his first role at the age of six, in a school production of *Peter Rabbit*. He began his career as a stage actor with the Cain Park Theatre in Cleveland and later performed for two seasons with the Cleveland Playhouse. Since that time he has had tremendous success in motion pictures and television and continues to do work on the stage. More recently he has added film directing and writing to his many achievements as an actor.

*Tell me about your early childhood and what special role you played in your family.*

My father did not speak English. He could write only his name and doing *that* took about seven minutes. I remember that we all had to be very quiet when he signed his checks.

I don't remember being young but I remember looking at a photo album of me and seeing a picture of me eating a hot dog. I was a very fat baby, very loved. My mother had three children who lived. Nick, my oldest brother, is now selling cars. She then had two children who died and then she had my sister Antoinette, who is eight years older than me. So I was really babied. My brother was better at school but I found that with charm I could get a lot more things done.

*Did you have aunts and uncles who were special? Were there large gatherings or events?*

I had a few aunts and uncles, but they were in Italy when I was growing up. Every time the family got together I was always the youngest child so I didn't do much talking. My cheeks were pinched a lot, as I remember, and my relatives seemed to get a lot of pleasure out of doing it. I learned that if I kissed old people they felt very good, so very often I would run and hug and kiss my older relatives. They would often speak Italian to me, and even though I didn't know what they were saying, I was sure it was something nice. It was terrific being mothered and caressed by all these people.

I remember doing things all together with my family, like making wine. My father was a very demonstrative man who yelled and screamed a lot—particularly at my brother and sister—in fact, he yelled and screamed until he got older, then he turned out to be a terrific guy, sweet! Nice to think about! I was the only one who was able to mimic him. When he was his angriest I would imitate him and make him laugh and then I could turn the situation around. It was as if I was playing gently with a lion. He was really a tyrant but I found I could manipulate him pretty easily to get what I wanted. Then as he got older, when he did something that was wrong for him, like climb a tree when he was seventy-five years old, I would use his old tone of voice and stop him. I would just scold him like *he* was the baby. I know that he really loved that because he knew I really cared about him. I find that making people laugh is really very important. My father also supplied me with my "Dominic the Great." My imitation of him led to that character I play in my nightclub act. [SHOWING BELONGING]

*Did you entertain your whole family?*

Yes. When I was with the big family I was very quiet, but when I was just with two or three people I would use whatever happened in the family, even if it was serious like a funeral, and they would laugh when I duplicated what was going on. So I entertained my mother and sister, making them laugh a lot by just repeating what happened during the day.

*What do you remember about elementary school?*

I was not the best student in the world; I know that. I tried really hard with spelling; it still confuses the hell out of me. And I remember how I passed Spanish one time. We were learning how a cow could walk about a well and make water come up. So I got twenty-five pounds of plaster of paris to make a well and a little cow, painted in blue and green, constructing the scene of this cow drawing water. It worked. I passed Spanish!

I remember that I fell in love with the art teacher, Miss Jenkins, because she had blond hair, which I had never seen before. And I got a very good mark in art, too!

*Did you participate in any school plays along the way?*
Absolutely. The first thing I was in was *Peter Rabbit.*

*Do you remember whether the teacher picked you to play or did you volunteer?*
I remember a play about Thomas Jefferson. We all took rolled cotton and made wigs with a black bow in the back. I myself didn't have a speaking part and Dominic Bimbo played the lead. But he was sick on the day of our performance and the teacher was stuck. I told her I knew his part and stood up and recited his entire speech. The class cheered, and I got to do it that afternoon in the assembly. I was thrilled.

Then I went to junior high school and joined the drama club and I consistently played the role of father, or some authority figure, being bigger, and was called "Father" then by fellow students. I was always very silly and got a lot of attention that way. One time we did "A Christmas Carol" and I played Fezziwig, a very successful rendition of a Santa Claus character. The next year I wanted to play Ebenezer Scrooge but everyone said I was too silly. I recall our drama teacher, Miss Semkin, sitting me down and letting me audition for this serious role of Ebenezer Scrooge. That was my very first script. I still have it. Here I was, a *round* kid playing Scrooge. But when I came out to take my bow the audience cheered; they didn't laugh. I was really proud of that!
[EXPERIENCING DOING]

*Was anyone in your family in the entertainment field?*
No one in my family was ever in the theater. My father was a garbage man and would bring home old pots and crushed typewriters for the metal.

*Did you go into sports?*

No. When I was twelve years old I had rheumatic fever. As a result of that, I couldn't go to gym class. I had restricted activity; I couldn't play hard. It also got me out of the army.

*Did your father come to see you in a play in school?*

He was always very supportive of everything I did. And I learned a lot from him. Sometimes people get annoyed with me because they think I pay too much attention to what is happening on the set. I'm not casual about my work. I'm silly at my work but I'm really there, paying a lot of attention. My father paid attention to us, and was right there. He didn't drink or go out a lot with the boys. Oh, once in a while he went out and shot a deer but he brought the meat home to us and said "eat."

*When did you know that you were going to be an actor?*

Two junior high school teachers, Mrs. Murdock and Miss Semkin, were very supportive. They told me to apply to a high school—Performing Arts, a new school that was opening connected with the Metropolitan Vocational High School. I was only fourteen and had to audition. My brother told me to do something from Shakespeare. So I memorized "All the world's a stage," but that part of the audition didn't go very well. Then I had to improvise, reading a letter. I said, "Dear Dom, you'll never get into the High School of Performing Arts if you don't pass the audition." I was very sincere as I remember, but they laughed and I passed.

*Do you have any contacts from that high school?*

There were people like Herbie Gardner, the successful playwright, Pat Crowley, Suzanne Pleshette, Joseph Wishy, who is at the Metropolitan Opera, Bob Ellison, producer/writer for Mary Tyler Moore. I can't think of all the names, but a large number of alumni from that school are all successful now.

*Did you develop serious acting or comic ability there?*

I became unique. I was not known in that school as a dramatic actor although I always had the potential to be so. But I found that getting laughter would be my thing.

*Did you practice your routines, making notes or scripts for yourself?*

No. I'm very spontaneous. If I feel safe, I can then be funny. So my job was not to be funny; it was only to make myself feel safe.

*Did the people in school become your friends? Did you hang out together?*

Oh, yes. Ken McMillan, Sheila Copeland, Bob Ellison, and I would just go out and play and laugh and be silly. We had a small group of people who stayed together. Because Jill Andre was in that school, I got my first job. Jill Andre's father, Marvin Klein, was doing an outdoor theater, a huge two-thousand-seat summer stock place in Cleveland, Ohio, called Cain Park. I went there to be stage manager.

Then I began to get little parts. I remember once I got a very hoarse throat from playing the lion in *Wizard of Oz*. The audience went crazy. Some of the reviews from that were terrific. I saved those early reviews. But the next week I couldn't talk so they gave me a part that didn't require talking. I got a lot of laughs in that show, though, because I invented a sly little laugh which I used for years. As a result of being there I auditioned for the Cleveland Playhouse and went there for three seasons. [RISKING LINKING]

*How did you know to go?*

The people from the Cain Park Theater encouraged me to audition. There was no money but I needed a scholarship. They paid me twenty-five dollars a week to work my ass off. And so I worked as an apprentice for two years. Within a year I was playing leads there, but in the beginning was very willing to do any kind of work. When they said pick up the couch, I ran and picked up the couch. When they said build scenery, I did. I was *always* eager and willing to do any job there, not just act! As I remember, I had just as much fun carrying the scenery as I did acting. [SHOWING BELONGING]

*Were you taken under anyone's wing?*

Frederick McConnel was the head of the theater. One night while everyone was walking out after doing *Stalag 17*, I walked up to him, put my arm around his waist and asked if he had any suggestions for my work in the play. All the apprentices couldn't believe I'd even touch him, much less talk to him. I didn't know he was untouchable, and he liked me very much for having done that. He gave me bigger parts as a result of my friendliness, I think.

*How did you know to do it? Had you ever made special relationships with other coaches or teachers?*

I used to have long talks with my biology teacher, Mr. Dorfman, with Mrs. Gore, my geography teacher, or Mrs. Mittenzwi, who just passed away. She was a big strong wonderful strapping woman who came to my father's funeral. It was nice to have attention from grown-ups who cared!

*What kinds of plays did you do with the Cleveland Playhouse?*

I played a real range of parts in *Hamlet, School for Scandal, Stalag 17, Best Foot Forward, Guys and Dolls.* When I was at the Cleveland Playhouse, I usually played parts that were composites of 80 percent of the character and 20 percent me. People had said they loved my work because they couldn't tell it was me; I didn't walk or talk like me. But that didn't sound right. So I tried playing 80 percent me in the next show, *Best Foot Forward.* And the audience screamed. The change in formula worked, and I still use those proportions. [EXPERIENCING DOING]

*Tell me about some of your other early experiences in the theater.*

A voice in me said, "Don't push yourself. They'll know." But when I was eighteen I auditioned for a show in New York called *Wish You Were Here;* the audition call said they wanted "swimmers." I went to the audition, lined up, but they didn't pick me. I left the stage, went into the balcony, put on my father's old bathing suit with straps over the shoulders, and took out a big book, on the cover of which I had printed "HOW TO SWIM." Now I stood in line with the rest of the people in their bathing suits. They asked who I was and then said, "Dom De-Luise, put your clothes on and get out of here." I didn't get the part but I made the *Daily News* the next day. "Death of a Salesman" was the title of the article!

It sounds very gutsy but it was frightening to me. I thought, in fact, that I'd never make it. I realized that this was not how to do it. After that I just went to straight auditions in New York. For instance, I was working with Dick Hoh on a nightclub act. It took us months—we got up every day to put together "Dick and Dom." It was pretty funny and we got a job at the Showplace, which Jim Paul Eilers owned. Eileen Brennan was singing there with Joanne Beretta and Mama Cass. We got two beers and dinner each night plus twenty-five dollars a week. And we filled the place with appreciative audiences.

*Did any connection come from this first act?*

Rick Besoyan, who had written and directed *Little Mary Sunshine*, used to come into the Showplace and drink. He saw me and asked me to go into *Little Mary Sunshine* as Corporal Billy Jester. So for one year I was in a very successful off-Broadway show with Eileen Brennan. [RISKING LINKING]

*What kind of other jobs did you have to support yourself?*

When I was twenty-one, I took baby pictures for a dollar each, selling house to house. I used my own 35-mm camera, and drove in every climate in my Mercury that my brother sold me. And when I didn't get work in New York in the theater, I would clean cars for my brother. I hated cleaning cars and still do. I'll bet I've compounded and Simonized a thousand cars. I don't clean my car now. And with Ken McMillan and Herbie Gardner, I also sold orange juice when Uta Hagen was doing *St. Joan,* and during *Guys and Dolls* and *South Pacific.* I made three dollars a night plus all the orange juice I could drink but I got to see those wonderful plays—every night. [EXPERIENCING DOING]

*How did you go about finding theater work in New York?*

I made rounds for two and a half years. I would get up at eight in the morning, go into the city, and go from one agent's office to another, giving them my picture. Ugh!

*Any luck?*

Max Richard had an office on Fifty-seventh Street with a little low window in the wall. You had to bend down to slip in your picture. I went there every week for such a long, long time. One day, in the elevator going down, I met a man crying because he'd finally gotten a job after having come to Max's office for four and a half years. And the job was as an extra in a movie. I knew right then that this was not how to do it. So then I started my night-club work which led to *Little Mary Sunshine*. I also started acting lessons with Sid Walters and Sid Lumet. Later I got a job from Sid Lumet who is now a very fine director. In High School of Performing Arts he was one of my early teachers. I submitted my name to Lumet when he was doing a movie called *Fail-Safe* with Henry Fonda. This was a serious movie about the destruction of the entire world, not a comedy. I learned the script, a part requiring me to give technical information with emotion. When I read for Mr. Lumet I remembered from school to recall something "personally devastating" which helped me deliver the lines with tears in my eyes. I got the part. I was and am very proud of that. [Risking Linking]

*How can you keep audiences laughing night after night with the same part, as in* Little Mary Sunshine?

I knew I had to keep working on the part, refurbishing it to keep it alive. If I didn't keep it fresh, I stopped getting laughs. I had to remember what my character's wants were; I really had to keep that *clear* in my mind; otherwise the laughs would leave. So I had to be *internally true to myself*, even though I was a comic performer, or it didn't work.

*So audiences really know?*

They absolutely know. The best performance I ever gave was when I had a fever of 104. I *had* to concentrate because I was deathly ill. The audience screamed; I never got such big laughs. I realized then that the more you concentrate, the better it is.

*What about the critics?*

They never reveiwed me in *Little Mary Sunshine*. But Bruce Geller and Jack Urbant produced *All in Love*, an off-Broadway musical. It was very British and I was a country bumpkin fop. The critics raved, "Comic genius." I started believing it. It turns out you shouldn't believe what you read about yourself because I later believed something that was awful and it knocked me for a loop. From "comic genius," I got invitations to lunch from all the agents I was trying to see while I was making rounds before the reviews. I realized they had to come to you. I'll bet I had eight or ten lunches at Sardi's, eating my way down the whole menu. I went with Jack Hutto, a literary agent, who brought me into William Morris in New York.

*Had you tried to get the critics' attention before?*

It never occurred to me. I thought they'd be too busy. But when they saw me in *All in Love* they thought I was great.

The next show was *Half Past Wednesday* and I played a very soft, sweet king who was so poor that his throne became a Murphy bed. And the critics said, "Another comic genius performance." I did "Mr. Fix" in *Around the World in 80 Days* at Jones Beach.

The third show wasn't so successful. This was something thing Jeff Harris and Bernie Kukoff wrote: *Another Evening with Harry Stoones*. In it was a girl named Barbra Streisand, as well as Sheila Copeland and Diana Sands. We were all doing our best. The reviews said Barbra Streisand was good and Diana Sands was terrific and I was very nice. Barbra immediately went on to do *Funny Girl* and I went on to do *Student Gypsy*, which Rick Besoyan, who had written *Little Mary Sunshine*, had done. With me were Dick Hoh, Mitzi Welch, now writing for Carol Burnett, Eileen Brennan. Rick was desperate for money so I invested in show business. I gave him all I had from the bank, five hundred dollars. The next day the show closed. This was the first time I was without money. Then the worst happened. Burt Shevelove, the director of *A Funny Thing Happened on the Way to the Forum*, was doing a play called *Too Much Johnson*, a turn of the century comedy with Nancy Berg. At one point the director had me turn toward the audience, look up in mock horror, and leave. Walter Kerr wrote that "Even Dom DeLuise felt it was necessary to make goo-goo eyes at the audience." Make goo-goo eyes at the audience! I had just been called a comic genius a year before by four different

critics. "Goo-goo eyes" was devastating! I decided that
Walter Kerr didn't like me, and I started to really get
depressed. I couldn't eat; I had chest pains, and I thought
I was having a heart attack. I had "anxiety," but I didn't
know a thing about psychology and really suffered for it.
I finally realized I had to come to terms with my anger
and that I had to recognize that critics are not gods. After
all, sometimes I am a comic genius and sometimes I am
not. Walter Kerr's few words made me collapse but I
was *very* collapsible. It took me all of two months to
start feeling like a person again.

*What was your next move?*
I auditioned for an already going Broadway play,
*Here's Love,* a musical of *Miracle on Thirty-fourth Street,*
for a seven-minute part of a psychiatrist examining Santa
Claus. For the first time I went to an audition in a very
*businesslike* way. I did the audition straight and figured
out a little bit where I put my eyeglasses under my tie
and then as I put them on it brought the tie up in front
of my face. I was very surprised when I got the part! I
opened on a Monday night with a show already in progress. I was stepping into an existing production. When
I did my scene the audience screamed with laughter.
Everyone in the chorus came to the stage to see what I'd
done. Later, I had to just walk across the stage and the
audience applauded. I really had a very small part, and
at the end, when I took my bow (I was one of the first)
the audience went crazy. Here I was, not feeling very
well, but *working* and the work was a godsend. Fred
Gwynne from that show was a very good friend to me at
that time—a prince. Then I got my first phone call from
England from Carol Arthur, calling to say, "Hi, remember me? We worked together in summer stock." She, Ruth
Buzzi, R. G. Brown, and I had done a show in Province-
town, Massachusetts, with Jerry Herman, who later went
on to write *Hello, Dolly*! Isn't it amazing how many successful people I met on the way? Anyway, she had gone
to London and called me from there. I was so flattered.
Later she became my wife.
Carol broke her arm in England and came back to
New York in a show called *High Spirits,* starring Bea
Lillie. She was on Fifty-second Street and I was at

Shubert's Alley on Forty-fourth Street and we were dating each other at that time. I was living on Fifty-fifth Street, so, since my show let out earlier, I would stop and see her last scene and then we would go out. Then Garry Moore saw *All in Love* and asked me to do his television show. At that time Ruth Buzzi was playing at Plaza Nine, a little club downstairs at the Plaza Hotel. I went there after my show and we wrote out a routine on four shirt cardboards to do on Garry's show. [RISKING LINKING]

*During any of this period was your agent getting work for you? Did you have a good relationship with Hutto?*

Yes! I found out that an agent could be a friend. Until this time they were remote; they just signed contracts. I didn't know that a good agent was as hard to find as a good wife.

Anyway, Ruth Buzzi and I got together and I used some of my father's angry Dominic the Great sketch for Garry's show. The audience loved it. Now in my comedy there was a lot of anger; anger which I was now able to release. The audience was screaming "Bravo, bravo." It was magical. This was the first time I had done big television and it was a huge success. Carol Burnett was very kind to us. We were invited to come back and do the same thing again three weeks later with Durwood Kirby, Carol Burnett, Garry Moore, and Eileen Farrell. It was wonderful. Bob Banner, producer of the *Dinah Shore Show,* was putting together a show called *The Entertainers,* to include Carol Burnett, Caterina Valente, Tessie O'Shea, Bob Newhart, and a couple of newcomers named Jack Burns, John Davidson, and Dom DeLuise. The last three of us were the *apprentices of* that show.

Then a wonderful thing happened. In the first show on the air, Carol Burnett and I did a blind date sketch in which I had a great part. The television critics called me a "wonderful, incredible comic." Their praise expanded my scope enormously. For starters, my salary went from three hundred to three thousand. But I was lonely. I wasn't married. I was doing television shows with audiences screaming, and I was going home to Fifty-fifth Street with a meatball sandwich and a Coke and watching the show on television sitting on a secondhand thirty-five-dollar chair.

*Tell me what you did to make contact with your audiences.*

When I walked on the TV stage I tried to sneak to my place to do my part before the cameras were on. Yet every time I tried to sneak to my place, they would cheer and applaud. Then I realized they could see me and that I had to get into my party mood as soon as I walked out. They would cheer and say, "Hi, Dom." They were nice enough to cheer; I should be nice enough to acknowledge it. I realized I *had* to respond to them instead of ignoring them. From those television shows, I learned that the audience wanted recognition, and I gave it to them. Such spontaneity was not only acceptable but perhaps essential, so I began using it.

Once someone came up to me to thank me for giving her husband some joy during the last days of his life. Years later I remembered feeling really terrible myself and being uplifted by something Steve Martin did on TV and I said the same thing to him. I know that comedy has a social value, that I am making an important contribution. I know I have that power and I love to use it. It is sensational for me to hear a crew laughing at eight o'clock at night after working twelve hours straight. It's a gentle life-giving gift that I am very grateful for. [SHOWING BELONGING]

*Are you playing the role of host to the world?*

I guess so. My aim is to make them feel comfortable and safe. Well, maybe not the *whole* world.

*Did you acknowledge other actors, comedians, directors? Were you actively supportive? How did you show it?*

I was always supportive. For instance, when we started out together on TV, John Davidson and I laughed a lot together. Triva Silverman is now a big TV writer but then we would work on sketches for four hours at a time just after we had worked eight hours at a time on the show. We had a terrific time together. When I wasn't working, I would be in the wings applauding and laughing for other people in the show. [SHOWING BELONGING]

*Did you have any special relationship with the directors at that time?*

Now I do—but when I was younger, no. That was like another world to me. I would thank writers for writing with me. I always took the time to thank them; even if I see them today I remind them of the sketches they wrote for me during that time, 1965, and about how brilliant they were. I recall so many, like Tony Webster, Pat McCormack, Mel Brooks, Bob Ellison, Neil Simon. For example, Dave Panish was one of the funniest writers for me. His words in my mouth make me look like a genius. He wrote an insane character for me: a psychiatrist who reassures his patient that there's nothing to fear. Then he sees a bug on his desk and screams hysterically. It's a sketch character but gets a big reaction from the audience because it clearly stated that sometimes a doctor can be sick.

*We must be up to 1965. What was happening in your career?*

I was working with Carol Burnett and Caterina Valente in a big television show when I got a telephone call from Doris Day in Los Angeles. She had seen me on television and wanted me to do a movie called *The Glass Bottom Boat*. I was ecstatic. The television show served as a movie audition for me. When I got to Los Angeles, I actually drove into MGM into my own parking space. Doris Day was so dear and good to me. The first day on the movie I could hardly speak and she was very supportive. She made me feel safe—thank God!

*Was this first movie a turning point for you?*

The television show actually was the turning point. The movie that brought me for the first time to California was *The Glass Bottom Boat,* directed by Frank Tashlin, who did a lot of the movies that Dean Martin and Jerry Lewis were in. In it were Arthur Godfrey, Dick Martin, Paul Lynde, and a lot of other comedians. We were all very supportive of each other. Movies are a very loving business. Here I was an unknown actor. Doris Day, for example, was especially kind to me. She used her power to make me feel at home, safe and appreciated. She made me brownies, which I never ate. I cut them up and saved them as "relics." You know, Doris Day brownies are hard to come by. I learned a lot from her about spontaneity in front of the movie camera.

You asked me if the picture was a turning point. In a way. Walking down the hallway of NBC, I met Kevin Carlisle, a former dancer from Cleveland days, now choreographer of the *Dean Martin Show*. He introduced me to Greg Garrison, who really changed my life. Greg asked me to prepare four minutes of comedy to audition for the Martin show. I had purchased a piece of material Carol Burnett didn't want; I literally picked it out of the waste basket and paid the writer $150 for it. It was about a bank teller who gets confused and mixes up his words —all spoonerisms. I took the material, went to my hotel room and from Friday through Monday I worked endlessly. I did the four minutes and all the secretaries laughed. Greg said I was terrific, and he would call me. He called three months later for me to do thirteen weeks of the *Dean Martin Summer Show*. My agent at William Morris, however, advised me against doing it. So I left my agent and did the show. [EXHIBITING SPECIALIZING]

*Did you immediately find another agent?*
No. I worked without an agent for a while.

*What has been the quality of your relationships with talk show hosts?*
Absolutely terrific. Johnny Carson did something with me four years ago when I was first on his show that people still talk about. I was using raw eggs on his show but told him not to worry; it wouldn't be messy after I saw how well dressed he was. He winked and then on camera started to throw the eggs at me and down my pants. I retaliated by throwing them back and spilling water over him. Burt Reynolds, watching it all in the Green Room, came out squirting whipped cream at both of us. It was spontaneous slapstick. The audience screamed.
Mike Douglas is wonderful. He thanks me by letter every single time I'm on his show. And he's already said he loves me in his book! He tells me that I'm the best co-host he's ever had and that when I'm there, he doesn't have to work. He calls me "a dream come true." When somebody tells you that you're a dream come true, you start thinking that God is on your side. [EXHIBITING SPECIALIZING]

*Up until this time would you say that any one person played the role of a mentor for you?*

In a way, Merv Griffin. On his show I had a chance to perform material I had written. It was like my learning period on TV talk shows. [USING CATAPULTING]

*How did you get to him?*

I don't know. I was the first guest ever on his TV show. I broke the ice and got a couple of laughs. Then Carol Channing came on. This was all on his first one-and-a-half-hour television show. In truth, I was terrified. In order for me to work on those shows I would have to sit in a bathtub for an hour so I could be very calm. I recall once I had just gotten out of the tub when I got a call. Someone was unable to do the show and they asked me if I could substitute. I got right back into the tub and sat for an hour, then did the show. Merv Griffin was very, very helpful because I did then what Steve Martin did on Johnny's show . . . a training ground.

*Did you support younger talent then?*

About four years ago I did write to Steve Martin to tell him that I was crazy about him. I wrote to Parker Stevenson when he did his first movie. I also wrote to Lily Tomlin when she was just coming into her own, playing the little baby. I think she appreciated my encouragement. I thought her work was brilliant, and I told her. [MAGNIFYING ACCOMPLISHING]

*Did you hear back from her?*
Of course!

*Did you hear back from Steve Martin?*

I met him on the street and he thanked me! Now when I go visit him he tells me I'll never know how important my support was. There's another bright new comedian I saw on the *Tonight Show,* Bobby Kelton, who I called up and encouraged. He was incredible. We're becoming friends.

*Have you received many letters from others whose encouragement was significant to you?*

The first time I was on the *Tonight Show* with Johnny Carson, Burt Reynolds was also on. The next day I got a hand-delivered note, "Dear Dom, will you please leave me alone? Love, Burt." I loved it. What support! Later, after doing *Silent Movie*, I met Burt in Florida. He had a script for *The End* that he wanted *me* to do. He said I was the only person who could play the part. He's always been kind to me and my family—my wife, my kids, and even my mother. I have seen Burt with vast numbers of his fans, and they are very aggressive sometimes. He has never, not once, even under his breath or when they are away and out of earshot, ever complained about being interrupted or bothered. He is *unconditionally* a terrific human being.

I also have many other kinds of letters that I treasure, from Hubert Humphrey and Pearl S. Buck. After Pearl Buck's letter, my wife and I got involved in her wonderful foundation which supports the children of American soldiers and Asian women, children who are rejected by both cultures. We had had three sons of our own and thought we'd adopt a little girl to support through the Pearl S. Buck Foundation. We contribute on every occasion that we can. [MAGNIFYING ACCOMPLISHING]

*Have you written others, to show appreciation for their efforts?*

Let me tell you about three letters I sent that were important to me because of the answers I got!

I recently saw *Foul Play* and wrote a letter to Chevy Chase, to Goldie Hawn, and to the director Colin Higgins. Originally I had been asked to do the movie but turned it down because I was busy. I was so glad to see how wonderful it was. They all responded with long letters back, which meant a lot to me. It was a terrific movie and I was very touched that Colin wanted me to be in it.

Most often I don't have to write. With performers I work with it's like having a ready-made family. I invariably go into their dressing rooms and we talk about our work.

*What kind of homework do you do?*

I do a lot of homework. For instance, to prepare for the *Dean Martin Summer Show*, which followed *The Glass Bottom Boat*, I hired Bob Ellison, who I went to high school with. He's now the executive producer of the

*Mary Tyler Moore Show.* He and I sat and wrote twelve sketches, for each of the twelve shows I was going to do. I came completely ready each week to do my own hunk if they needed them, and they always did. I paid him two hundred for each sketch.

*Were there others at this time who were particularly helpful to you?*

Sure. Dean Martin was always wonderful to me and my family. I had an eight-year relationship with him. During the time when I was doing the *Dean Martin Show,* I got a call from Jackie Gleason. He invited me to come to Florida to do seventeen shows for him. I was thrust into the Gleason world like a child into the lion's den. I was stepping into a big man's shoes. Gleason really did everything. In his stead, I gave menus as well as directions about production. It was hard because I was so young. Those seventeen shows were terrific. I even edited them. Gleason was so sensational just to give them to me to do. One of the most thrilling experiences in my life was to be in a room with Jackie Gleason and Bill McCutchen. Gleason worked with us for four hours and he taught me to pay close attention to the details of a scene. His detail work was gorgeous. I loved it when he told me that I reminded him of himself when he was twenty-five years old.

I couldn't even talk to Dean Martin when I first met him. I remember my first sketch with him and my mouth went dry. The audience didn't laugh. Greg Garrison called me to Dean's dressing room and Dean grabbed me and hugged me, throwing me down on a chair, saying he was just like me. He made himself available to me. He made me feel safe. I did the sketch again. This time the audience screamed with laughter. I worked with Dean for eight years after that.

On the *Dean Martin Show,* I became friendly with everyone. I found that the bigger the people were, the sweeter they were. By sweeter I really mean easier, kinder, more dear. Jack Benny always put his arm around me and called me Dommy. I loved him. Jimmy Stewart and I talked endlessly about life. Lucille Ball called me the funniest young fellow she's ever seen and recalled a cowboy sketch I'd done—in detail.

You never know about anybody, though. I recall doing

the *Glen Campbell Show* at CBS and talking to the card boy, someone who holds the cards to cue us, about his wife and problems, eating and life in general. I had many conversations with him. One year later I was on the show and saw him. Assuming he was still the card boy, I asked him about his family, as usual. He answered and then called everyone to attention. I was startled as I realized he was now the director of the show. I hugged him and said, "Bravo! Good for you." [USING CATAPULT-ING]

*You did theater, TV shows, a movie and all this before 1967. Did you ever replace your agent?*

I did have another agent, Merritt Blake, then I married, started a family, and moved to California to this very house. I was doing more movies, grew to be friends with Greg Garrison, and had a very important meeting with Mel Brooks. First, through a friend, "Winky," I met Anne Bancroft, who was doing the movie, *The Slender Thread,* with Sidney Poitier. I couldn't believe that she had asked to meet me, let alone knew who I was. One night, standing backstage at *The Devils,* a play she was doing with Jason Robards, she introduced me to Mel Brooks. He invited me to do a movie with him called *The Producers,* but I couldn't do it. Then he started to do *The Twelve Chairs* and had me meet with him for four hours in his Beverly Hills Hotel bungalow. We talked about our lives, our families, nothing to do with show business at all; it was just life-sharing. He offered me the part of the priest if Peter Sellers turned it down. Mel said Peter Sellers was worth a million dollars and I was worth only one Thom McAn shoe. But regardless of what happened, he said we'd always be friends. And of course, as things worked out, I did do the movie. We worked very hard for six months in Yugoslavia. The picture was terrific for me. He went on to do *Blazing Saddles* and hired me and Carol; then I did *Silent Movie* with him. And now I've done *Fatso,* written and directed by Anne Bancroft.

*How did she choose you for this film?*

I had told Anne stories about my family over the ten years of knowing her. In particular, I recall telling her about my father's deathbed. The family was crying in one room and eating spaghetti in the other. Bereaved, we still finished the meal. She eventually wrote a story weaving all my little vignettes around a character called Dominic Napoli, who is very much me. She's written a love story about a compulsive eater. She's starring in it with me, playing my sister. I could never have written it because I would never have thought that people would be interested in my eating habits. But the crew working onstage say that they alternately cry and laugh and are quite moved by it all.

*Are there any other cycles or patterns that you see in your career?*

When I was younger, insecure, and frightened, I was too afraid to admit that I was ever angry. When I could admit that, I found I moved ahead in my career. I realized I didn't have to be funny all the time, that in fact I could be serious. That was a breakthrough. From playing Scrooge as a little kid, I could now direct a movie called *Hot Stuff*. I was in charge of a hundred people with a budget of two and a half million dollars.

*How do you account for this last change?*

I met Howard Rothberg, Anne and Mel's manager, who sat me down and together we planned my career. I was heavily involved in television, even with my own series, *Lotsa Luck*. He advised me to withdraw from television and accept only movies and nightclub work, acting and directing. Many offers came through from television and, incredible as it sounds, we turned them all down! I did some movies with Gene Wilder, whose influence was strong, starting with *Sherlock Holmes' Smarter Brother*, which we made in England. While I was acting in movies, I never ever thought I'd be directing them. When Ray Stark and Mort Engleberg asked me to read a script—*Hot Stuff*—for me to direct, I couldn't believe it. Carol read it first and gave me the okay sign and then I read it, rewriting about 30 percent of it and putting in as much warm feeling as I could. Suzanne Pleshette, Jerry Reed, and Ossie Davis, along with a new actor, Luis Auplos, are in it. Suzanne went to high school with me; Jerry was on the *Glen Campbell Show* with me. Now it's done and up on the screen. And I got a big kick out of doing it! [USING CATAPULTING]

*What did you learn from directing?*

I realized that I can get a lot out of actors. When an actress's lips quiver from fear, I know how to put her at ease—complimenting, teasing, appreciating her. I have a lot of power to make working together a happy and terrific experience. When things get tough, I sing or dance with someone from the crew. I know it sounds silly but it all serves the purpose of putting people at ease, making it safe, and getting the best work out of them and myself. There was a lot of love. I work the same way with my kids.

*Speaking of your children, do you take any care to train them or see to it that they have any special experiences or skills?*

My wife and I agreed to do things together as a family. For example, when I do any woodwork, I see to it that hammers and nails are available to them so that they work along with me. When they make something for me, I use it. We are tremendously supportive of their learning to take care of themselves. Now they are overly helpful. When I drop something, everybody bends down to pick it up. We are all helpers. My youngest gets to help with family suggestions too. When it's his turn, he picks where we all go for dinner. He usually picks Jack in the Box, not La Scala, but we all have fun.

Let me tell you one experience that was crucial for me. One son stole some shiny rocks from school and I went to see the principal for advice. He told me to take my son out for a walk and spend some time with him. He counseled me on dealing with all my sons; let them know I loved them, give them a job they can accomplish, and then listen and implement some of their suggestions. Such simple advice! Yet I have used it so successfully with my mother, my wife, my friends, my co-workers. If a lighting man suggests something, I listen; if it's good, I'll do it. That's the way I worked on *Hot Stuff*, and it worked. They all came forth with their ideas and their love. All I had to do was ask for help, point to someone who had given the idea, and say aloud it was good, and I'd have more and more from everyone. Their suggestions made me look even better, and I loved it. [SHOWING BELONGING]

*What are you working on now?*

I have a contract with the Sahara until 1981, if I live that long. I was officially welcomed by Buddy Hackett when I went out onstage at the Sahara in Las Vegas in front of a large audience. This well-known comedian, so well established in Las Vegas, particularly at the Sahara, took it upon himself to come to see me work and accept me in the Las Vegas area and into his own home. He just sent me a book he'd written, inscribing it, "And the Lord said, let the comedians be friends." He reached out to me, and I must say I was very touched. [SHOWING BELONGING]

In fact, I'm doing more work now than I've ever done in my life. I just finished the Muppet movie, and *The Last Married Couple in America* with George Segal, Natalie Wood, Valerie Harper, and Dick Benjamin and *Fatso*. I'll do some more nightclubs in Reno and Denver, at huge salaries. It's incredible. Now when I perform before thousands of people, I do what I want. I don't have to worry about them laughing; they laugh. I had an argument one night in Denver with a man who felt I was bothering him. I took ten minutes to tell him that I wasn't trying to embarrass him but only to make him feel good. I love my work and I want to do it well. The reason I'm here is to entertain people, to make them laugh and to rejoice and celebrate life with them. [EXHIBITING SPECIALIZING]

*Have you had any special awards given to you?*

Yes, Father of the Year, which was simultaneously given to Gerald Ford. And I have gotten the Humanitarian Award from Notre Dame in Boston, which was also given to Carol Burnett and Pat O'Brien. And the key to the city in Miami, Florida, which, by the way, has opened *no* doors for me. [MAGNIFYING ACCOMPLISHING]

*What are you working on now?*

I'm writing a film story for the first time. It's about a guy like me with a wife, three kids, and a dog, who feels trapped—imprisoned at home—and then gets into trouble and goes to a real prison. The theme of my movie is that maybe the life we all have ain't so bad. Enjoy it. I've never been to prison, but I have an appointment to spend some time there and get some input. I was recently very impressed by *Scared Straight*, a documentary about lifers giving so much to youngsters to keep them out of jail. I cried so hard at their love and power and poetry. Then too I have more directing projects. And of course I want to lose weight!

# CHAPTER TWELVE

# John Brooks Fuqua

John Brooks Fuqua is the chief executive officer of
Fuqua Industries, Inc., a business conglomerate of extraordinary dimensions. He is a self-taught man whose
difficult childhood didn't prevent him from building an
empire. He has also served his state, Georgia, as a state
senator and a congressman, and has been state chairman
of the Democratic party. At one time he had a close relationship with President Carter, who has referred to Fuqua
as his mentor.

*Let's look back to the beginning of your life. I'd like
to ask you some questions about kinds of activities, pursuits, and relationships that may have been pivotal or developmental to what you do now as one of today's most
successful businessmen. Were you part of a small or a
large family?*

My mother died when I was three months old and I
was raised by her parents. My parents also had another
son six years older than I, but for all practical purposes
I was raised as an only child.

*Did you work when you were very young? Did you go
to a regular school?*

We lived on a small tobacco farm and everybody
worked. I went to a country school.

*Were there such things as extracurricular activities
aside from basic subjects in which you participated?*

There were sports, of course, but I didn't participate in
them at all. But there was also debating. I found it to be
extremely useful in later life. I can today get up and
speak before ten people or ten thousand people without

being nervous. It all came from the training of a simple country high school in debating. I remember that they had many contests every week. I don't recall whether I won or lost; I guess I won some and lost some. Nevertheless, the training was invaluable. Another thing that was helpful to me at that time was the senior play. Country high schools had what they called the senior play whether they had enough seniors or not. For the last four years of high school, I was in the senior play every year. And that type of exposure also helped me overcome the typical problem that people have in being hesitant in getting up before groups. [EXPERIENCING DOING]

*Do you recall how you got to be in the plays?*
I must have made myself available. I was asked to be in them. I know it was something I was interested in.

*Did you go to college? I know that you read a great deal.*
I am questioned frequently about which college I went to, but I never went to college. From time to time in making talks I would explain that while I never went to college, I really did get a comparable college training. I found out when I was thirteen years old that I could borrow books through the mail from Duke University, which was about seventy-five miles away. Duke had a huge library and the post office had a special book rate that made it practically free. So I borrowed every book I could on matters relating to financial and economic matters that could never be available to my country high school. Sometimes I'd read a whole book and only understand one chapter. But I read a lot of books and learned enormously.

I've repeated this story a number of times to different interviewers and, after seeing it in print in the early Seventies, the head librarian decided to check to see if it was true. Sure enough, he did find out that I had borrowed lots and lots of books. I have hanging in the office an honorary doctor of laws degree that was awarded to me from Duke as a result. [RISKING LINKING]

*How did you first start reading these books?*
First, I just was interested in it. The other reason was that I saw in the county seat that the people who had the

most influence and affluence were bankers. I decided that if I was going to get out of the economic environment that I was in, then the only thing to do was be like them.

*Did your grandparents encourage you?*
No, but they didn't discourage me. But that's what I did, developed a great interest in financial things at a very early age.

*Did you then start working in or developing any small businesses?*
No, but it was my objective to do that.

*What did you do at sixteen when you graduated from high school?*
Before graduation I had become interested in ham radio. That was even before I had ever seen a ham radio station. But I got the books and read about how to make one and I got the parts and put them together. Then I had a ham radio station and had, in hand, at sixteen when I graduated, a first-class radio operator's license, the highest license you could get. The first job I got was as a radio operator with the American merchant marine. I, of course, had to be eighteen, but they didn't look at the records too closely. I fudged on my age and was the youngest officer in the merchant marine, I guess. [EXPERIENCING DOING]

*How did you think to apply to the merchant marine?*
When I took the examination to get the license, I asked the man how I'd go about getting a job. He told me to go down the street to RCA that hired the radio operators for the American ships and make an application. Well, I went down there, even though I had never been in a big town before, and I did just that. Sure enough, one day I got the telegram delivered to the little village that was nearest the farm which somebody then had to bring out. It said that I had a job in the merchant marine as a radio operator. I then worked at it and saved all my money. In a year and a half, I got a job as an engineer in a radio broadcasting station in Charleston, South Carolina, and subsequently in Columbia, South Carolina, in another station owned by the same people. In six months

I was chief engineer of the second station. [RISKING LINKING]

*What did you do to move so fast?*
I just did what one does. I was a hard worker and tried to impress the boss. I demonstrated that I had technical ability and ambition. I wanted to do something more than what I was doing.

*Let's talk about ambition for a moment. I've found that although people want more, they don't know how to demonstrate their specialness, or anticipate things, or develop opportunities from problems at hand. They just work harder. And wait. I'm sure you didn't just work harder and wait. Can you say anything about those extra things that you did which nobody ever reveals?*
Hard working itself is often thought of as only physical work. If it were true that hard work alone did it, then my yard man would be one of the wealthiest people around. What I did was find out what the manager of the radio station did. So I spent much time hanging out with him and the other people who were involved in the management end of the business, rather than the technical end. I found out what they were doing and thinking. By the time I was twenty-one, I felt I knew as much as the boss did and could do as good a job as he did. [SHOWING BELONGING]

*Did the manager then give you extra assignments when he saw your interest?*
No, but I did them anyway. Then what I did was decide to go in the business end of the broadcasting business. After all, it was all I ever wanted to do. So I then did what would now be called a marketing survey to determine where another radio station could be built. I picked out three places, which I could support with figures and various other factors. One was Augusta. [EXHIBITING SPECIALIZING]

*Did you get any assistance or advice from anyone?*
No, I did it all on my own. I hadn't, as a matter of fact, ever seen anything like this done before nor had any method to use except common sense. I knew how to play around with figures as to how to get revenue, and

how much it cost to operate, what the profits ought to be, how long it would take to recover the loan, and things of that type. I learned it from the time I had started reading books when I was thirteen, and then I learned firsthand when the boss would let me see the figures so that I knew what was going on. It wasn't very hard to figure out what it cost anyway. I knew what everything cost and what everybody made, and I figured I could certainly determine what other costs were. Once having done this, I made a presentation to what would be potential investors. [EXHIBITING SPECIALIZING]

I went to Augusta, Georgia, to the Chamber of Commerce. The secretary of that Chamber of Commerce saw me. I told him that I thought Augusta could stand a second radio station. While I didn't have the money to build one, I did have the know-how to operate one and make it profitable. I had a lot of self-confidence. I asked to be put in touch with somebody who had some money and ambition to do something about it. He did it and put me in touch with some people. Subsequently, we got a license to build the station and I was given ten percent of it for putting it together even though I didn't have any capital to put into it. I became manager over a small staff. That meant that I sold advertising in the daytime and wrote advertising copy in the evening. Sometimes I did some of the announcing. It was a small operation, but it was successful. [USING CATAPULTING]

*Do you think you were lucky?*

You can influence luck. If you want to get more from the sunshine, you don't stand on the north side of a tree; you stand on the south side. Now there was the case that if that secretary of the Chamber of Commerce had not been there, if he had not seen me, nor taken any interest in me and what I wanted, or if he hadn't known whom to call, I would not have been successful in that town. I'd have gone on to the next one. But he was there, just the kind of man to be interested in helping young people.

I later became president of the Chamber of Commerce just so I could give this outstanding man a pension, which he did not have. I wanted to fix that, and I did. He had done so much for the community. Furthermore, in his final illness when he was old and forgotten by the young generation of businessmen, I paid his hospital expenses and his funeral expenses. I had an opportunity to pay him back, but he did more for me. People ought to appreciate what others do for them all the way along. But people mostly just don't do that; they just take things for granted. [SHOWING BELONGING]

*How was participating and leading the Chamber of Commerce helpful to you?*

It gave me a more prominent image in the community and gave me an opportunity to help solve some of the problems of the community and to exercise some leadership. It was just that kind of job.

*After your radio station, what was your first business venture?*

I learned about the value of courage. You cannot make it on your own. You must use other people's money. The way to do that is to establish credit. I began to establish credit initially by buying a lot and having a house built on it; then I'd sell it and make a small profit. I'd turn around and buy another lot. Then when I needed more money, I'd be able to borrow it because I had proven myself.

*Did you know your banker before you went for a loan?*

Yes. It was a small town, and I knew everybody. Well, not everybody. I knew all the leaders of the business establishment. I looked for opportunities to make some money and to multiply the money I made. The first big money I made came through a friend of my wife's and mine, a lawyer who came to dinner one night. During the course of the evening, he remarked that the man who owned the local Royal Crown Bottling Company was eager to sell the business but was in a dilemma. He couldn't get his money out because he had accumulated a great deal of money in his corporation. He needed a tax break. By eight o'clock the next morning I was in that man's office because I knew enough about taxes and his situation, if my friend's story was correct. Sure enough it was, and the man was eager to talk about selling. And sure enough I took his money out of his bank account and bought his business with it. Three years later I sold it for a hundred-thousand-dollar profit and that gave me a fairly good amount of capital and other business. [RISKING LINKING]

*Did you depend on advice from anybody?*
No assistance from any financial associates. I then started buying and selling businesses. For instance, I bought a wholesale bakery business, the biggest mistake of my life, but I bought it. It was not wise, but I learned. I began to accumulate experience and got to know people in larger companies. I also joined the Young Presidents' Organization.

*Let's talk about that organization. How did you first join?*
I joined it when I was thirty-five years old and of course had to get out when I was forty-nine. Then I became interested in two or three groups that stayed on past the age limit. It has been extremely valuable to me over the years. I have made so many business contacts that I now know a wealth of people from all walks of business life and have known them all these years. It's been very helpful. I can't say I've made any money from it, but that is not the point. The fact is that it has been significant. [RISKING LINKING]

*Can you say more about its effect when you first joined?*
I decided I was as smart as these other guys were who had big businesses. I always did have confidence; at my age now I see it is sometimes based on not a great deal. But nevertheless I decided I could run one of these big companies as well as they could. They didn't have any more knowledge than I had. Certainly they didn't have any more courage. So then I decided I would look for a company that would be the basis for a large business operation. And I began a search for annual reports and other kinds of financial information. I spotted one day, in reading a whole annual report, an over-the-counter company which on the assets side of the balance sheet showed that it owned twenty-five percent of Natco which was on the New York Stock Exchange, an old brick and tile manufacturer. And on the liability side, it owned the same amount as the assets side. Additionally, the officers

of the company endorsed the note. I looked up everything and knew it was something that I could just about
afford, if I could get the right banker.

I first went to see the people and they were willing to
sell. Then I went to the banker, long since passed away,
who created this First National Bank where I have these
offices. He understood instantly, whereas others I had
gone to never understood what I was talking about. After
I told him my story, he said that the only reason I was
going to get this deal was that he hadn't seen it first. He
loaned me two and a half million dollars to buy control
of that company. And I did. We moved that company
from $14 million in 1965 to close to two billion in sales
this year. That basically is my business experience. I
made a lot of capital in twelve years and invested and
reinvested it in various ways. By ordinary standards, today I'm very substantial, and I have outside interests that
are far greater than the value of my interest in this company.

*Let's talk about your involvement in politics for a
while. There are other rich men who never would run or
who run and don't make it. Why did you run?*

Certainly politics has been one of the most valuable
experiences in my entire life. I gave the ten best years
of my life to it. While it was all on a part-time basis,
it took a lot of my time. I was in the House of Representatives for three terms and the Georgia State Senate
for one term. I was in the Senate when Jimmy Who had
just been elected to it. As a matter of interest, I was just
in Washington recently at a party with Jimmy Carter
when he told everybody I was his mentor. [MAGNIFYING
ACCOMPLISHING]

*What's behind that?*

I helped him a little. He had less experience when he
came to the State Senate than I did. I was the state
Democratic chairman and I felt an obligation to new peo-
ple. I went out of my way to help him learn the ropes.
Help of this type just should be given. Of course, I didn't
know that he was going to be President of the United
States; I'm sure at that time he didn't know it either.
[SHOWING BELONGING]

*What motivated you to get into politics?*

I was a real doer in civic things. I tried to give back to the community a portion of what it had given me. I gave it back in supportive jobs and in elected jobs. I supported a lot of solving of civic problems. Also I saw some of the candidates for the House of Representatives of that county not of the quality I wanted to see; I was a little idealistic perhaps. I wanted to see things done well here.

*Did you have a good chance in your first campaign?*

How can I explain? Well, I was the only businessman running against lawyers.

*But you must have had to persuade others to support your candidacy. Who did you go to?*

A few friends helped me. I decided how long I was going to be in the legislature and I knew I was going to be somebody. Now, when you get to be somebody, you have to get to the governor. The governor had already been a pretty good friend of mine.

*How did that happen?*

I just knew him. I always knew all the governors and all of the presidents since I've been thirty. I've always been named to serve on committees. My best friend was in the Senate and wanted to be governor in 1962. I decided that if he wanted to be governor, I'd help him be governor. But he was as unknown statewide then as Jimmy Carter was nationwide when he ran for President. First there were two of us supporting him. So I went to the bank and borrowed one hundred fifty thousand dollars on my signature to get the campaign started, and before we got through, we got two-thirds of the total vote. I myself served in the Senate two years of his four-year term. I had enough and got out because I wanted to get along with my business. At that point I determined I wanted to be in bigger business like this. I obviously couldn't do both. [SHOWING BELONGING]

*Please say more about how you got to know the governors.*

I just made it my business to know them. For example, I went to see them at the state capital. I went as a citizen and a businessman. I talked about almost anything. People in this state just do that. If you're in business and interested in getting things done, you certainly ought to know the governor if he has any power at all. In Georgia, he has substantial power. So that's how I did it.

*Did you continue to help Jimmy Carter after you left the Senate?*

He served two terms in the Senate, only one term while I was there. When I dropped out, he ran for governor and got elected. I was not very close to him. But I helped him as much as I could in his campaign for President, though we all laughed at first when he said what he wanted to do. He did call me in the beginning to get my help in his running for President. It was all I could do to keep from asking what his mother had asked, "President of what?" But I saw he was serious, and I asked his scenario and thought he didn't have a chance in the world. He didn't even have the forum of being in the governor's office any more. But I didn't discourage him, and as I recall, I took him around to several of the officers here and introduced him as the next President. [MAGNIFYING ACCOMPLISHING]

*Does he call for your advice on any issues?*

He does send emissaries from time to time when he has certain problems that I might help with. But I am not active in the Administration.

*What kinds of people would you say you have reached out to, to help open doors or make ways possible?*

There are so many that frankly it would be immodest for me to say. I get a genuine joy out of doing something for people. I'll give you an example of my personality. At my television station in Augusta, Georgia, the Friday night after Thanksgiving, I gave a party for everyone who had been with the television station ten years or longer (some had been there thirty). I gave each one of them a thousand dollars—not a bonus or a thousand dollars to pay taxes on, but a thousand dollars on which I had already paid the gift taxes so that they could blow it all if they wanted.

*So you were rewarding their loyalty to you?*

No, not loyalty; appreciation. I do things like that out of deep appreciation for what they've done for me. But you can't buy loyalty with money. You have to treat people fair and proper. I do it every day with all of my business. Here in this office throughout this company which has twenty-five thousand employees, I do it by treating everybody alike, fair, and try to compliment them on a job well done. The fellow who just interrupted us on the telephone just reported in on last month's fabulous results and I told him how well he'd done. I do it because I think that's how it's done. That's what separates the men from the boys. Most people don't do that. We're all different personalities. But some people really don't appreciate what others do for them. [SHOWING BELONGING]

*What do you answer when people ask how you have been so successful?*

I remember talking to high school kids who always ask how you succeed. Success in itself is a relative thing. What I say is, first I hire people who are smarter than I am and I motivate them to use their talent. Then I use other people's money. It's just that simple.

*What happened to you after you left the Senate and went back to devoting yourself full time to your business?*

It was the time that I started looking for a company to become a vehicle for a large cover company. I planned this company to be what you'd call an international corporation. I borrowed enough money to buy control of it. It was on the New York Stock Exchange and I developed it from about twelve million dollars to about three billion dollars this year.

*Were you doing anything else at the same time?*

Always. I don't recall specifically, but I had a number of other business interests and also personal business interests. I've always stayed busy, but personally that's not a plus, if you were to list my pluses and minuses. I don't have any interest in games, sports, or anything. Consequently, I'm sixty years old and have reached a point where, if I were to become disabled or be forced to be retired for some reason, I'd be miserable. I'd be lost. I'd strongly recommend to other people that they never get themselves into this kind of situation.

*You don't take any vacations?*
No. Well, it may be what others will call a vacation; I'm going to Florida the day after Christmas. I'm going to stay a couple of months in our home down there. Actually I work there because, in my particular job in a company this size, it really doesn't make any difference where I physically am. The company does not hire me for my muscle but for my experience and leadership.

*Do you and your wife continue to have the same friends all these years or are new ones added?*
It's some combination of both.

*Do you have any close friends, or confidants? Are you different from the majority of men who have never developed these close relationships with other men?*
I didn't expect you to make that remark. But you are more right than you know. I fall right into that category; I have very very few real close friends.

*Do you tell those close friends those things that trouble your heart?*
No. Only my wife, perhaps.

*Is your son in business with you?*
Mark is not connected with Fuqua Industries. He is in private family business.

*Do you have anyone here in Fuqua Industries whom you think of as a son and treat that way? Does your business become a family?*
No, I don't. It becomes a family in the sense that I enjoy a degree of warmth, and have all my life, and I cannot explain why, other than what I've said about being fair to people. I have always operated differently from any of the executives of any big business that you'll find. They depend on their professional management and bring in board members from outside. Here we use our own people. [Magnifying Accomplishing]

*Do you hire people specifically with college degrees or do you want something else?*

I can't answer that completely because I don't personally hire people. But as a basic rule, we do at corporate headquarters hire almost entirely law graduates and M.B.A.'s. That doesn't mean that those are necessarily better qualifications but, as a general rule, that means they have had the courage and stick-to-it-iveness to have gone ahead to add years to their education which should pay off down the road.

*Your own childhood was one of hard work, but work with real consequence and contribution to your grandparents. Did you want the same for your son? I would guess that he never would have to work for his living. Yet did you encourage him as a boy to work or make any contribution?*

Yes. When he was fourteen years old and we were living in Augusta, I insisted that he work in one of my television stations. And he did. He was interested in it and it was very good for him.

*How do you identify and reward talent and bring people up in your company? How do you bring people up to manage your subsidiaries?*

We try as little as possible to bring in outside people. We try to develop our own people. Of course, there's an argument to be made on both sides of that. Right now we are faced with changing presidents. Our chief operating officer has been president of this company for nine years. He's my age and the company has grown to where it's too big for him. We're moving him to another area where he can contribute. We need younger people, brought up in this company, who are anxious to run. So they're going to have a chance.

*Do you spot people and encourage them?*

Yes. We spot people primarily to bring them up, and one of the things that I do is encourage them. It's so easy to do it. It's so easy when you come in in the morning to even say good morning to the receptionist; it's so easy to compliment somebody who does a job nicely. I've done it at least twice today. It's so easy to do and it's proper to do it.

*In addition to that positive good feeling, how do you bring some talented people along, those whom you think are worth extra investment? Can you think of one specific person whom you coached to expand or continue . . . ?*

It's really difficult in a company as large as this; we have small contact. It does become more and more difficult with more and more people. I just complimented someone on the  phone who had just done a fine report. Well, that is his job to do that. What he did was no more than he was supposed to do. But I complimented him because he did it well.

*Tell me what the signs are that spell ambition.*

One has to be impressed by long hours to some extent, but I am not necessarily so by those who stay here late at night working. Some stay because they can't get the work done; a lot don't want to go home anyway because they have unhappy marriages; some are like me and are night persons but don't come in early. I can't really identify what a better answer might be.

*Is there somebody you're especially proud of who's come up and been helped by you?*

A man who holds one of the most responsible positions in the company, the vice-president and controller, who's in charge of all the numbers. He's been with us a good number of years, and he began by finding unusual numbers and unusual analyses. I encouraged him to do more of it and I paid him a lot, in the seventy-five-thousand-dollar range when he was only thirty-three years old. I could have ignored him or just accepted his work without saying anything. But he might have lost a lot of his enthusiasm. I think the failure of the employee is the employer's fault, not to recognize and give proper credit. [MAGNIFYING ACCOMPLISHING]

*How can you account for knowing and practicing this? I've heard that you consistently receive awards, like the Boss of the Year.*

I enjoy a degree of almost fanatical warmth in whatever business I'm in or whatever I do. I'm often asked what I consider that is different about me from my peers and I have thought about it. My answer is that I have more courage to do anything than anybody else. That sounds like bragging in a way, but I mean it very sincerely. I don't have crises, but I have a lot of courage. My observation as I have gone along in life is that the world of people would be so much better if they just had more courage.

*Tell me about your work with Georgia State University.*

I've always been interested in Georgia State University. You can see it out the window; it's right down the street. It's an interesting school. It's got twenty thousand students, half in the day and half at night, with ninety percent of the students employed. It's got one of the best business schools in the country.

*How do you contribute to it?*

Money. Sometimes I go down and give lectures to the graduate business school. It has become good because the president sold the state a long time ago on having a top-notch business school here. He got them to pay professors the same way they pay them at Princeton or Harvard. He needed money to do that but, being a state school, you have a scale to pay professors so that Professor A makes the same at one school as Professor A at another school. So he worked out a plan to get the private business community to put money in the pot so that he could get a superior grade of personnel.

I've done some outside things too, like last Friday and Saturday I participated in a board of trustees meeting. I'm also on the board of a smaller boys' college in Virginia operating over two hundred years continuously. The contrast between those two schools makes it a right interesting thing. We have some of the same problems but the way they handled them is so different. In a big university with top-notch leadership like Duke, the president runs the school. He makes the decisions and knows what he wants to do. He has the board of trustees meet four times a year and go through his plans, but he has already decided what's going to be done. Everybody knows that. The little school up in Virginia is different. They never have forgotten how I sat there for two hours one day and finally said, "Well, gentlemen, I've listened to you talk about wine and women for about as long as I'm going to listen to you." Imagine. They were upset about whether girls could stay in the dormitories with the boys on which nights, and for how long, and whether they could bring whiskey to the ballgames. It was just a totally different world. [MAGNIFYING ACCOMPLISHING]

*Did you make any impact on changing them?*

I guarantee you that I changed that school like it has never been changed. I finally had the board of trustees come down here in this office and said, "Look, you run an educational institution but you're spending all your time worrying about boys and girls being together and whether someone's going to drink some whiskey. That's not your purpose. Your purpose is to run an educational institution. The best way to get rid of the other problem is to wipe out all the regulations. If you just do away with them, half of what the students claim they're doing now just won't happen. When something is no longer prohibited, it won't be nearly as attractive. The drinking part will drop in half." So they wiped out all the regulations. And it did. That was my way of solving the problem.

*When you reflect over the past decade of the changes you've made, would you say you are more or less social?*

I'd say I'm less social, not because of the change in my personality but by the mere demands on my time. I just don't have the time to be socially active. I do a great deal of traveling. Sometimes I think that the worst thing that ever happened to us is the corporate jet. We have three of them sitting out in the hangar all the time, so there's no excuse not to go somewhere.

*What happens on that jet? Do you travel alone and work?*

Most of the time I read. Sometimes my wife travels with me.

*Do you still read what you used to—financial texts?*

Yes. I read balance sheets far more than most people do. I see opportunities in buying other companies more than my peers see because they don't read. People ask how I found out how to buy the latest acquisition and, nine times out of ten, we found it ourselves. I have one employee whose sole job is to read annual reports and to tell me about the interesting ones.

*Do you write letters or telephone people whose accomplishments you appreciate?*

I do a great deal more of that than my peers. Today I dictated at least a half a dozen personal letters . . . Jim Horinda, J. Pritzka of the Hyatt Theaters, the former Secretary of Agriculture. I do a great deal, always have. The person who receives such appreciation is impressed and remembers. The problem I have with the schools is that they don't teach communication—how to communicate, one person to another. The average graduate of an M.B.A. course does not know how to write a business letter nor how to make a good and efficient and productive telephone call. I'm on the board of visitors of the business school at Duke University. They don't understand me, but the dean does and I harp on it all the time. You got the whole list of courses, but not the first single course in communication skills. I tell you that ought to be one of the most prominent things. It's how to communicate ideas, how to take a minimum amount of time to communicate thoughts. I also wish schools could teach how to communicate one's appreciation to great people who have made contributions. [SHOWING BELONGING]

*Have you thought about writing?*

No, I haven't. I'm not an eloquent speaker. I tend to be critical of writing. And when you're critical of writing, you tend to think you must write better than the person who is writing. So I haven't written anything of significance. But maybe someday. I could make a contribution with what I know, about how to get ahead in business. Townsend, who had been the head of Avis, wrote a best seller, *Up the Organization.* I think I could do a book of that type; it fills a real need.

*What about other books you're impressed with?*

Well, I do run across many interesting books. In fact, I order the most impressive ones for my corporate officers and one or two other people in the various subsidiaries who I think would be interested in them. I buy a lot of business books and pass them on. For example, Malloy wrote about how to dress for success a few years ago.

That book contained some of the best advice you could get anywhere, and I sent it all over our company. There have been so many books. One recently was a very impressive little pamphlet about the oil crisis. Now I know from my firsthand experience with gas and oil that there is more crude oil in this world than we'll ever have to use, and it pains me to think of the politics of that. It's hard to believe that the American people have been so bamboozled about a crisis. While I don't want to get off on this topic, let me just tell you that I was impressed with this little seventy-five-page booklet. I wrote to the author, complimenting him, and I ordered about two hundred copies for my officers. [SHOWING BELONGING]

*Do people respond to you when you send them books?*
No, not really.

*Doesn't that bother you?*
It would make me feel better if they did respond. But I have to remember that most things are taken as a matter of course.

*What are your future goals in business?*
I'm going to start all over again. I have no outside interests or hobbies so what I have recently done is to buy control of a closed-end investment club which has about sixteen million dollars in cash equivalent and thirty-three hundred in stock and a listing. When I retire, I'm going to start all over again. It's going to be my retirement to start over.

# CHAPTER THIRTEEN

# Judge Shirley Hufstedler

Judge Shirley Hufstedler is the U.S. Secretary of Education. She was formerly a U.S. circuit judge of the Court of Appeals for the Ninth Circuit. She began her career in private practice, became a Superior Court judge in 1961, an associate justice of the California Court of Appeal in 1966, and was appointed to the U.S. Court of Appeals in 1968. She has been very active in her profession, and was named Woman of the Year in 1976 by the *Ladies' Home Journal,* and has received many other awards and honors.

*When you were a child, was there a particular role you played in your family? Were you expected to do one thing versus another thing? Did you, for instance, play cards with the family or read aloud with the family?*

Yes, we did all of those things. There were conflicting signals in some respects. My mother was a person of German heritage who believed in running the place like a German drill sergeant. It was expected that I would achieve a great deal intellectually, study hard, get good grades. The other message was that it was necessary to obey the power structure. That was very much a part of it. I very early decided I would render unto Caesar that which was Caesar's but I would keep my head to myself, so I worked out my own negotiation about what things I was willing to go along with, what things were demanded by the overall society and by my family in particular, and what things I was going to do in my own head.

*And your father?*

He did not figure enormously in this kind of negotiation. I adored him. He was a very charming, witty man and very warm and outgoing. He also had his difficulties. He was so absorbed in his own demanding business, general construction, that he really spent very little time with me when I was young. We did, however, have very pleasant times on holidays and trips and other special occasions, but I can't say that he was a dominant factor in my decision-making, except to the extent that he impressed upon me in many ways that it was essential to have a good education and that success in any phase of life meant an awful lot of hard work and practical application. In his opinion, business was critical and all this stuff about literature and teaching was really not to be taken to heart. On that aspect I didn't take him too seriously, but I did as an undergraduate fulfill all of his dictates and get a degree in business administration. That's what he wanted me to do and I did it. But I was never under the impression that that was what I wanted to do with my life. I did that to please him. Then I did what I wanted to do.

*Let's talk about what you did in high school—your activities, roles, how you recall your thoughts about your relationship to the high school milieu.*

My social life in high school was almost nonexistent; I was going to have to make my own market, so to speak, and it was going to be a small one in any event because I was too young physically and too old intellectually to fit in at all in a high school scene. I thought the whole thing was a nonstop misery from one end to the other, and I didn't think the program was intellectually challenging. I spent an enormous amount of time in the library, reading independently, and was interested in music and pursued that. I was a pianist. I also did the school newspaper thing, which I thought would be interesting and rather rewarding. [EXPERIENCING DOING]

*When you think about the newspaper, as an example of an activity, what did you do to fit in?*

I never thought about fitting in. One just went in there and worked. At that time I didn't have any preconceptions about relating to people. I got along with people quite well. I always have, primarily because I learned early on, as a kind of self-protective device, what things I was willing to yield to and what things I was going to fight about. I kept the reason to fight at a very very low level because provoking a whole bunch of useless arguments seemed to me like a waste of time.

*Were you also active in college in activities involving student dorms, clubs, councils?*

I was not a political activist as such. I followed the societal pattern at the University of New Mexico. I belonged to a sorority and was active in student affairs of various sorts. I was the business manager of the newspaper. I participated in some intramural sports. [EXPERIENCING DOING]

*Then, after you graduated, what did you do?*

I went to work as a private secretary for Paulette Goddard and Burgess Meredith.

*How did you get to do that?*

That's a complicated story, but I can abbreviate it this way. I had become a very dear friend of Ernie Pyle. He was a great World War II correspondent who had been killed in action, and when one of the studios decided to make a movie of his war experiences Burgess Meredith was hired to play the role of Ernie. Burgess came to New Mexico when I was there during the war and I became acquainted with him. By a series of extraordinary happpenstances I had been offered a job, which I was about to take, with an advertising agency in Los Angeles. One day I was having lunch with a friend at the movie studio and ran into Burgess. He offered me a job. He was then married to Paulette Goddard. I hesitated in hopeless indecision for about two minutes because it offered me about three times what I was going to be paid at the advertising agency and I wanted the money to go to graduate school. So I took the job. [RISKING LINKING]

*How did you know what you wanted to do?*

Actually it was a very pragmatic approach. Primarily I knew what I didn't want to do and that excluded a great many things. I decided very late that what I really wanted to do was go into medicine, but by the time I came to that decision, I had invested too much time in other directions. It would have been very difficult to start over again. So I then looked at what I'd shown some talent for versus what I'd already invested time and effort in and decided that since I had already shown promise in undergraduate law I'd go to a good law school. [RISKING LINKING]

*How did you choose the law school?*
Here again it was a combination of circumstances. I had been very attracted as a youngster to the beauty of the Stanford campus, and it had an excellent academic reputation. It also happened that an old friend of mine who had been with me as an undergraduate was applying to Stanford, so I applied too; it was really rather unplanned in the ordinary sense. Of course a lot of law schools that I might have considered wouldn't have been open to me, and some of them that were I couldn't have afforded. So I went where time and circumstances led me.

*Why were some not open to you?*
A number of law schools didn't admit women at all. Remember, this was 1946. Harvard and Yale, for example, didn't admit women until 1952 or 1953. The choices weren't endless, and I was relatively comfortable with the California schools. Of course, some of the present law schools weren't even in existence then—for instance, UCLA Law School.

*Were you the only woman?*
No, there were five of us in the entering class that year. It was the biggest class that had ever been admitted to Stanford because it was the first class right after the Second World War. They even ran double sessions. The place was flooded with returning veterans. There were two of us who remained for the full graduate school program. Very few women applied to law school, not because of any policy of exclusion on the part of the university; they just didn't apply.

By then, Carl Spaethe was the dean and was the moving force in founding the *Law Review*. I was selected for the *Intramural Law Review* at first, which was the predecessor of the *Law Review*. Then Volume I, Number 1 came out when I was a senior. I worked on that intensively. The experiences with the people on the *Review* were an enormous influence on my life. Not just slightly, but enormously. After all, I married one of my fellow workers on the *Review*. [EXHIBITING SPECIALIZING]

*Can you be specific about these influences?*
In terms of sharpening writing skills; learning about a wide variety of avenues of inquiry; editing scholars who didn't do what they said they were going to do, or sometimes produced hopelessly unacceptable work; and developing the skills of being tactful enough to turn down articles scholars submitted. All of these had a great influence on me.

*Where did you actually work—in your apartment or on campus?*
The last two years I worked almost entirely in the *Law Review* offices. I did what class work I got around to doing there and did all *Law Review* work there too. [SHOWING BELONGING]

*So there was a lot of interaction with professors as well as students?*
Yes, in the early stages of the *Review* that was true because those who were, in effect, baby-sitting the *Review* to get the thing off the ground did work with us closely. The editorial decisions were our own, but we needed help. [USING CATAPULTING]

*Are you still in touch with any of those people?*
I keep in touch with all those persons regularly, corresponding and seeing them when I can. And the students who were members of the staff, in addition to Seth, whom I married, became and still are my lifelong friends.

*What did you do after graduation?*
I got married and looked around for a job. The number of people who were interested in hiring anybody, let alone a female lawyer, were few and far between. It took a lot of beating the bushes. I had an offer of a clerkship with the Supreme Court of California, but I couldn't take that because I decided to get married and live with my husband, who wanted to practice in Los Angeles. So I looked around here and eventually started in

a very loose-jointed way with a solo practitioner. That developed into an association and I stayed with him.

*How did you find him?*

I had a list of Stanford law graduates in practice in Los Angeles, and I started calling on each of them asking them if they knew of any job opportunities for me. One lawyer happened to need some work done right at that moment, and he hired me to do it. One task led to another, and I did more and more work for him. After a year, I left him and opened my own office. Although I continued to do contract work for him, I began developing a general practice and at the same time I was associated both with my husband's firm and with many other lawyers who hired me on a contract basis. [RISKING LINKING]

As the years went on, I continued general practice and did a good deal of trial work. Other lawyers would associate with me for the purpose of undertaking various stages of complex cases.

I began by ghost-writing briefs. Lawyers for whom I had done brief-writing began to associate with me for the purpose of drafting pleadings and motions. Thereafter, I was retained to argue the motions. This work led to an increasing number of associations for trial work. The combination led me to become a litigation specialist, retained by other lawyers. That specialization was responsible for my being retained as a special consultant to the Attorney General of California in the highly complex litigation in the Supreme Court of the United States between and among the United States and several states, including California, over the water rights in the Colorado River. I moved in and out of that case for about five years. The year before I was appointed to the bench, I worked exclusively on that litigation. [EXHIBITING SPECIALIZING]

*How did the Attorney General of California know you?*

Several ways. The person who made the initial difference was a professor who was a baby-sitter for the *Law Review.* He had, in the meantime, become Assistant Attorney General of California, then the second man in charge of the litigation for the Colorado project from California. We'd kept in touch, so he knew the type of work I did. [USING CATAPULTING]

*Could you explain how you kept in touch? Did you, for instance, initiate the correspondence with him?*

No, he did. Through him I knew the Attorney General, and the work simply went on. The then Chief Counsel, who was an independent person, was very much impressed by the earlier work I had done on a contract basis. So when the chips were really down, I was retained to go to work full time.

*And then what happened?*

I was appointed to the Superior Court of Los Angeles. Pat Brown had been the Attorney General when the litigation began and he was Governor of California by the time the litigation had ripened to that point.

*What were your moves then?*

There were twelve new judgeships created and I received one of them. With a newly created judgeship one must then run at the next general election. I ran at the next general election, unopposed, and was elected. I then stayed on that job for five years, although the final year I was sitting on the Appellate Department of the Superior Court, appointed to that job by Roger Trainer, who was then Chief Justice of California.

*How did he get to know you?*

Primarily through my opinions in the trial court, and by that time I had a large web of friendships among professional people who knew me and of me and what I did. [SHOWING BELONGING]

*Did you participate in any kind of activities other than your actual work to build this network?*

No, not to build the network. I participated in other activities simply because I thought it was the right thing to do. I worked actively in the then Women Lawyers Club, and I was president of that organization in 1956. It has now become the Women Lawyers Association. I didn't do that to make contacts in the sense of building a practice; I did it because I wanted to get acquainted with the women in the profession and I felt rather strongly that lawyers should contribute to the upkeep of their profession and do some kind of organized bar work. At that time the Junior Barristers was totally closed to women; they just didn't admit them. And while women were admitted to the Los Angeles County Bar, if just didn't turn out that any of them were appointed to committees that really did anything. That was a way to get involved with bar work. [RISKING LINKING]

Of course in the meantime I had had a baby and was undertaking to run a household and take care of children, a houseful of pets and all the other accoutrements.

I kept up all of my personal friendships with all kinds of people that I had worked with professionally, or who had been law school classmates, but in the sense of going out to build a network of contracts, no, I did not do that. The whole matter went primarily by word of mouth, I expect, through people with whom I had associated. [SHOWING BELONGING]

*When you look back over your career, how do you see your progress? Have you become a different kind of person? Has your role changed? Do you do different things?*

I never thought about my career in those terms. There were obvious markings along the way. I went from being totally unknown to having an excellent reputation for legal work on hard cases and knowing many, many people in the profession. That took a lot of determination and energy and production.

*Did you collaborate with your husband at all in your career?*

Yes, during the early years when I had my own practice. I opened my office in the suite in which my husband was practicing with his law firm. I developed an association with that firm, so that in addition to doing my own things I also worked on a variety of things for his firm. It was a very loose association that lasted for ten years. I was never an employee of that firm, but I was in the broader sense an associate all those years.

My husband and I enjoyed working together enormously and we did work on the same cases, not constantly but occasionally. We did so throughout our period of practice. It was great fun; I enjoyed it. We had wanted to practice together at the beginning but it was hard enough to get a job for each of us, let alone get a job as a package.

*After your career took off within the court system, did you decide to give up the working relationship? There was a point where you could have worked together. What made you choose the court system?*

We could have, but I thought overall he was getting all of the rewards that he wanted through law practice and his work within the Bar. He was very successful at all aspects of this and he did not have any great interest in going on the bench. I did. We've always had an extremely close personal relationship, but it didn't strike either one of us as odd that I would do the one thing and he the other. And we had, of course, worked very closely on matters with which both of us are concerned, in the areas of Law in a Free Society Project and all kinds of court reformation and reorganization projects. We had no conflict of interest from anybody's standpoint on that.

*It's very hard sometimes to point to specific skills or situations that were important because they are all a part of the overall pattern. It's only when there is a failure or a huge disappointment or some kind of bucking of the system that we can get to know the system and begin to know what skills were vital at some point. Can you think of any particular disappointment, great or small failure, that was a jolt in your career?*

I really cannot think of a particular thing. But all of the years of growing up, changing grammar schools sometimes twice a year all over the west, showed me that there wasn't a life structure into which I was going to fit. One had to make one's market, so to speak, every single day and every single time. There was no security in being able to drop into something and expect something lovely to happen. It didn't. So my expectations of employment and how I would be received in the legal world were all set against such a background. It simply never occurred to me that life wasn't going to be difficult, that getting jobs was not extraordinarily hard. That was part of the Depression experience. The idea that things were going to be simple never occurred to me. I expected it to be difficult. I expected to have to make my own way. I expected a substantial amount of rejection because that had been the entire pattern of my life. [EXPERIENCING DOING]

In the meantime I had developed my own sense of defense mechanisms so that I learned not to take all of these things personally. Those people did not hate me because I was a bad person or because there was something terribly wrong with me, but rather they were trying to live their own schemes in their own ways. Prejudice against women was unfortunate, but, like some other kinds of diseases, I wasn't smitten with the disease. I thought it was their problem, not mine. In short, I had simply learned to cope with it through myriads of jobs. I had always had a job when I went through school.

*What kind of jobs?*

I began working when I was fourteen years old. I worked at what I could get, a salesgirl in dime stores and department stores, I made surveys for statistical companies, going house to house, canvassing. [EXPERIENCING DOING]

*How did you find these jobs?*

Some of them I went out and aggressively searched for; some of them found me. I also worked as a secretarty; I taught music; I worked on newspapers; I worked in a mortuary. In short, I did anything and everything that came by that would produce money for me. I didn't have any money and while we were hardly impoverished in any general sense at that time, there simply wasn't anything left over for any extras I wanted.


*What is the typical career ladder for a federal judge? To move up the state system and transfer to the federal, starting at the bottom there?*

If there is any typicality, the most frequent federal judicial career ladder is for a person to be a private or public practitioner of considerable experience who then becomes a United States Attorney. As such, he or she is not only in charge of a district office of the Department of Justice, but he or she is also the chief federal prosecutor for that district. Many federal district judges have been appointed directly from their service as United States Attorney to a federal district judgeship. Many United States circuit judges were elevated to the circuit courts after serving as district judges. Sometimes the ladder begins in a state court system. A person who has been a member of a state court of last resort is appointed a federal district judge. He or she may thereafter be elevated to the court of appeals. In a few instances, a judge of an intermediate state appellate court will be appointed to the United States Court of Appeals.

*Did you career this way?*

I was a state trial judge, then associate justice of California's Court of Appeal, from which position I was appointed to the United States Court of Appeals.

*What do you think were the combinations of factors that catapulted you from the California Court of Appeal into an appointment to the Circuit Court?*

There were at least two especially significant factors. The first was that I had had the opportunity to demonstrate competence in both trial and appellate judgeships during my service with the state judicial system. I had not only had several years of experience as a regular trial judge, but while I was a member of the trial court, I had also been assigned to some of the most difficult departments of the Los Angeles County Superior Court, each of which carried huge caseloads, and the cases often involved very difficult questions of law. I had also served as a member of the appellate department of that court before I was appointed to the California Court of Appeal. These judicial positions required me to debate with a large segment of the litigating bar and to write hundreds of opinions, which gave my work a lot of visibility within the legal community. [EXHIBITING SPECIALIZING]

Of equal importance, however, I am a woman, and even a decade ago, there was significant political pressure to appoint qualified women to the federal bench. No woman was then sitting on a federal appellate court. Only one woman in the history of the country had ever been appointed to sit on a federal court of appeals— Judge Florence Allen, who was appointed by Franklin D. Roosevelt to the Sixth Circuit in 1934. Judge Allen died before I was appointed. In the decade of my service on this court, a significant number of able women have now achieved prominence in the legal community, and I am confident that some of the new federal judgeships will be filled by these distinguished women.

*Now I am deliberately going to ask about only your nontechnical competences—those so-called soft skills that none of us has really labeled before this time. I'm interested in ferreting out how you went about making alliances.*

I did not deliberately go about "making alliances." Rather, I have always had great interest in the human beings with whom I have worked, whether the persons are judicial colleagues or supporting personnel. I want to know them and to understand, as far as I am able, what they think about and what is important to them. As a Superior Court judge, I could have been a loner, but that role did not appeal to me. I wanted to participate in the work of the court as a whole, not only the work of the particular department to which I was assigned. I made it a point to go to lunch with the other judges regularly. The relaxed social occasion of luncheon is a way to present oneself in a collegial, noncombative professional structure. [SHOWING BELONGING]

The Superior Court judges' lounge made modest luncheons available. It was very easy to meet my brother judges, many of whom were senior on that court and were therefore in a position to make a wide variety of policy decisions. We could have a quick lunch in the lounge and still have about forty-five minutes to play dominoes, or cards, or chess. When you work with people and when you also play games with them, you find out how they think and behave, as anyone will attest who is a bridge or a tennis player. You may find that you do not know people very well until you play some kind of competitive game with them. You can also find out a great deal about people if you take a trip with them. You can discover the nature of their responses to stress and to many other things. The game setting brings out characteristics which you might not ordinarily see. Therefore, I played various kinds of games with my colleagues to get acquainted with them in a way that I believe was very revealing to each of us.

*Did you take a special role? For instance, were you the one who organized a card game?*

Early on I did not. I waited to be asked and when I was asked I very happily joined in.

*Did other women do the same?*
There were no other women. I was the only one.

*Did you deliberately play cards and lunch with colleagues to overcome any barriers?*
I did not treat lunch as a social way to go up the ladder. I did it because I really wanted to meet the other judges. However, it really did serve me. I did want to know what my brothers thought about and they were also very helpful. When I had a legal problem that was bothering me I could discuss it with a judge who had more experience.

*Your initial appointments both to the Superior Court and to the California Court of Appeal were by the governor. How did you get the governor to know you?*
The governor got to know me quite well through my work on the Colorado River project. He also knew my husband's partner, who was my sometimes associate. And, by this time, I knew many very distinguished members of the bar. I knew them very well and very favorably, and they knew me in the same way. [SHOWING BELONGING]

*Did you play an active part in professional associations? Were you, for instance, a luncheon speaker yourself?*
Yes, I did some professional speaking at lunches at that time. [SHOWING BELONGING]

*How did that happen? Did the speeches arise from cases that you were working on at the time?*
When anyone asked me to speak at the time I was working on the Arizona-California project I would. I knew a lot about the topic, and I would arrange the materials to present a professional lecture. And then, at the same time, while women were not permitted to join the county lawyers called The Barristers, at the State Bar there was another group of young lawyers who did not forbid women to participate and welcomed me. Also I volunteered to speak and in that way met a lot of young lawyers in my age group, lawyers who had occasion to work with older lawyers of the Bar on projects and programs of interest to them. I spoke on many professional

occasions, and as a Superior Court judge I did quite a bit of speaking to nonprofessional as well as professional groups. [RISKING LINKING]

*Did you have any special roles among these judges? Such as problem solver, for instance?*
Yes, that happened quite often. I was a negotiator and an accommodating person, that is, one who was able to assist someone who could not meet his calendar for that day. If I could move my schedule around for him, I did. [EXHIBITING SPECIALIZING]

*Is that unusual?*
Well, there were never very many people who wanted to volunteer, and I was one who did.

*Why did you volunteer?*
In part it was because I am an accommodating person and in part it was because I have always wanted to learn what was going on in the next department to forward my own experience. When people ask me to do something reasonable, I have a strong impulse to do it if I possibly can. That may be due in part to a duty-struck background, but I think it is a combination of other things as well.

I must emphasize that there is a lot of difference between being an accommodating volunteer and a busybody. In adapting oneself to a new organization, structure, or institution, it is usually counter-productive to offer one's services to someone who has expressed no need for anyone's help. The first step is always to learn the territory. What is the history, purpose, and function of the new institution? Who are the people within it and what do they do? It is remarkable how much one can learn simply by listening closely. Moreover, almost anyone will be glad to respond to polite questions asked by a newcomer who is genuinely interested in the person who is being queried. I underline that the interest must be genuine. Small children are not the only people who can quickly spot a glib phony. Only after one has an understanding of both the institution and of the people who are in it should a person in a subordinate or collegial role begin volunteering. People understandably resent newcomers who have very much to say before they know what they are talking about. Depending upon the size and complexity of the organization, the belonging process may take many weeks or even many months. [SHOWING BELONGING]

*I see that you have a very different sense of responsibility toward people than many people seem to exhibit.*

That idea seems very strange to me, but now that you identify it, I know it is true. I know it from my own experience. People simply have too many pressures and problems to want to put up with anybody who is always beating his or her breast with their frustrations and their single-minded causes. One just doesn't have enough energy to put up with people like that. There is a lot of difference between being supportive and being a doormat, and I can see that there are many people for whom that differentiation is never very clear.

*Do you think the way that you supported other lawyers and judges is different from the way that men do?*

Some men who didn't engage in supportive actions were afraid of exhibiting what they would call weakness. Some advice that I received a long time ago, which has been very useful to me indeed, is: If you want to make a friend out of an acquaintance, you ask him to do a favor for you—not a great one, but something the individual can easily do so that you are very modestly in the individual's debt. Now many people are afraid to do that because they are so fearful of rejection. If a simple request is refused, some individuals go into a funk for a week. Actually, the person saying no may have perfectly good reasons for refusing you without it having anything to do with you individually. But I have used that advice to advantage. [SHOWING BELONGING]

*Did you, for instance, write complimentary notes to or call your colleagues who performed exceptionally well in situations either at court or in professional meetings?*

Always.

*Did anybody do it for you?*

One person did once. And that made a difference to me and that taught me what to do. Now it's true that today I don't do it as much as I used to, but I still do it from time to time, especially when the person is young. But I never do it unless they've done an outstanding job. [SHOWING BELONGING]

*Have you made a difference in anyone's life to your knowledge as that one person made to yours?*
Yes, to one young woman who argued a case extremely well. I didn't write directly to her, but instead I wrote to her boss. I didn't even send her a copy of the letter. Now whether it made a real difference to her boss, I can't say, but I do know it made a real difference to how she felt about how she was perceived. She has made fine progress ever since. Occasionally I hear from her.

*Who were some of those influential people, even mentors, who helped you move up?*
There were many many, all kinds of people in various structures all along the way who gave me help. They did not perceive themselves as necessarily being mentors. Although some of them did, most did not. They were helpful and supportive to me because they were helpful and supportive people.

*How did you act to those who perceived themselves as mentors? Did you take a specific question to them or did you go for general advice?*
It usually wasn't that to begin with. I would have reason by the fact of my lawyering to see that person and then we would have, for that same reason, an ongoing relationship. I remember one man, who did not know me at all, who heard me argue a case. He only knew whom I was associated with. He picked up the phone and said to my associate, "This gal can sure get things done." He not only did a favor for the person for whom I had appeared, but he also was really interested in seeing young people who displayed great talent move up. He both wanted to demonstrate his friendship to my associate and to help me move up. [USING CATAPULTING]

*Did his praise to your associate directly help you?*
His comments about my talent made it practicable for me to move from my first association to my own office and an association with many friends. It gave me the courage to make the move. The confidence I gained was

also reflected in my professional work. He was a very well respected judge, very well known, a hard taskmaster.

*How else did he help you?*

We ultimately became very good friends. He really was a mentor who took very great interest in both me and my husband, making sure that each of us met the most distinguished lawyers in town. He organized lunches and dinner parties. We had an excellent relationship. We were very good friends and showed our affection to each other. I thanked him a lot. He knew that I appreciated him and I did.

*Were there any other mentors or those who played key roles in your life for a period of time or even intermittently?*

Many, all the time. There are so many people in so many different ways who have been kind to me, going out of their way to do something for me, that I could not even begin to name them. [USING CATAPULTING]

*Which are some of the boards that enhance or magnify your profession?*

I would hesitate to put it that grandly, but I do sit on many boards. Many, but not all, are charitable boards. You know I'm not permitted to sit on boards of for-profit organizations. For example, I sit on the Board for the California Institute of Technology, the Board of the Aspen Institute for Humanities, the Board for the Constitutional Rights Foundation. If you look at, say, the Board of Directors of the Aspen Institute, you can see immediately that there is no way that I can really enhance them. It's quite the other way around. It is one of the most distinguished boards in the world. I am the one enhanced. [MAGNIFYING ACCOMPLISHING]

*What did it mean to the legal profession that you were there?*

I can't say what it means to the legal profession; I can speak only for myself. My service on these boards and commissions has broadened my own horizons and helped me to keep touch with the developments in many other disciplines. It is my hope that by constantly learning, I may be able to bring greater insights into means of resolving some of the hardest problems that exist in our society. For many reasons, the most difficult and divisive problems rising in our pluralistic society are presented to the federal judiciary in the form of litigation.

It is not enough to have technical competence in the law to try to struggle for wise answers to hard questions. Nor is it enough to be aware only of developments in one's own country. Today we live in an internationally interdependent world, and the events in other countries have an impact on our own. In the judicial arena, massive infusions of litigation, and as a concomitant, intractable judicial backlogs are a way of judicial life not only in the United States, but also in all of the developed countries of the world. The litigation explosion has even reached many of the developing countries. Senior governmental officials in such diverse places as Nepal, Malaysia, and Poland are as interested as we are in trying to develop mechanisms for dispute resolution without resorting to litigation.

Thus, whether I am teaching a seminar in Austria, or working on a person-to-person tour for the United States State Department, I find that exchanges among my colleagues abroad are useful in trying to solve dilemmas that are familiar to us all.

The Aspen Institute has developed a host of major international programs, including an international justice program. These programs give me and others an opportunity to explore means of reducing tensions within our own societies as well as within the international community.

*Do you have professional time to do this or is it on your own?*

This is on my own. To have time to do these other things means that I do not have any leisure. I became used to working double shifts when I was rearing our son and my husband's and my careers were very demanding. After our son grew up, I had a lot of energy left over from my work requirements, but I was not willing to devote more of it to my caseload because it was too confining. I saw this time as an opportunity for development and intellectual growth. Therefore, I deliberately undertook invitations to join boards which will give me the greatest possible range of perspectives: one board with international, interdisciplinary objectives (Aspen Institute for Humanistic Studies); one excellent liberal arts undergraduate college (Occidental College); one outstanding educational institution devoted primarily to science (California Institute of Technology); one board concentrating upon our cultural and historical heritage (Colonial Williamsburg Foundation); one board of an institution that devotes its entire attention to scholarly legal work (American Law Institute); and two boards that serve as counseling bodies for law schools (Board of Councilors for the Law Center of the University of Southern California, and Visiting Committee for Harvard Law School).

The combination of experiences provided from service on these boards has been extremely rewarding intellectually and personally. The fact that such service means that my hours of work are extremely long and that I must forgo virtually all leisure activity is not a deprivation. At a different stage of my life I would not have considered it. Now the price is well worth it to me. [Magnifying Accomplishing]

*Do you think this makes a difference to who you are?*
I suppose it does, but I think it's probably more important with regard to the breadth of my interests than any one-to-one relationship.

*How did you choose your law clerks to whom you have an extraordinary reputation as mentor?*
For the two congressionally authorized law clerkships to which I was entitled, I usually received over two hundred applications from outstanding law students throughout the United States. The clerkships are for one year and they are awarded after the student has graduated from law school. Under my direction, my law clerks went through the applications and graded them. I checked the grades and thoroughly read all of the early applications to see if we agreed on our evaluations of the applicants. Thereafter, I read only those applications that my clerks had graded B+ or better. My former law clerks are spread around the country and I often used them to help me by doing preliminary interviews of promising applicants. Gradually I reduced the list of persons under consideration to not more than twenty-five, with whom I ar-

ranged personal interviews. After I had interviewed the candidates, I whittled the list down to five, all of whom were always dazzling. It was very difficult to choose among them.

To pick the finalists, I telephoned professors who were members of the faculty of the applicant's law school. If the professors did not know the candidate personally, I could count upon their doing some research and calling me back. Unsolicited letters in support of a candidate's application were sometimes candid and useful; but, more often, the letters were about as objective about the candidate as a letter from his or her mother. I had a few guidelines. I did not pick two students from the same law school for the same clerkship year. I liked to have a man and a woman. That did not always work out, but that's what I liked. I strived to choose people who would be complementary to one another, and both compatible and supportive of one another. Finally, I refused to settle for less than the very best. [MAGNIFYING ACCOMPLISHING]

*Do you have continuing relationships with your law clerks?*

All of them. They all become part of an extended family and I see them all over the country. They are very supportive of me and to one another. We worked very closely together because the work was hard and there was always too much of it, so they simply had to be able to work in that structure.

*How did you coach your clerks?*

I tried to coach them regularly, but primarily the clerks taught each other and themselves by doing the assigned work. I helped them by explaining why I accepted some points and rejected others. I meticulously went over their work and discussed it with them. Some of the skills learned during a clerkship translate well to the outside world. Thus, the process of critical analysis, precise writing and speaking are essential skills not only in judicial work but also in law teaching and law practice. Others, such as negotiating skills, can also be partially learned by watching and by listening to the interchange among members of the court about particular cases. [MAGNIFYING ACCOMPLISHING]

*Do you take vacations?*

I like going abroad and doing things there which are as significant and challenging to me as what I do at home. Simply taking a trip down the Rhine doesn't do all that much for me. I am fond of walking in the Himalayas; I go there often with friends, judges, and other lawyers. We have all kinds of things to talk about, maybe about the scenery or cameras or law or restructuring this or that, or we may be talking to the Sherpas, what's happening to their social system as a result of Western culture.

*Do I dare ask you anything about the near future of challenges for women?*

Well, I think women are here to stay! I don't know if I can say anything that hasn't been said. I am seeing women being accepted in large, prestigious law firms. But it has taken a lot of time and there are a lot of leftovers both from the standpoint of the employer as well as the employees, both of whom have hard times. But the situation is changing. One thing that is happening for women who have begun a career and who are now in their thirties is that they are having second thoughts; somehow they had thought that all of life's problems would be worked out by making a particular career choice, and that, of course, is simply not so. As you look at life, you see the problem is that it's so *daily*, and it doesn't become less daily as you become older; no matter what you do there are some options that are foreclosed to you even as others open up. Those women who really thought that things would be resolved by choosing a particular career are disappointed.

I might say for those women who've decided to be homemakers all their lives that they come to different career choices as well, because they find that that particular course may not be adequate. I'm in hopes that both women and men can look forward to a little more time to talk together. It would be a very pleasant thing, though I don't think it will happen soon. People are going to have to get over the urge to put hair shirts on for their own decisions. The amount of guilt is terrible. People simply cannot work together with others if they are substantially disapproved of or substantially proven wrong. Women are criticized so much of the time that a lot of them learn to stay back. We have to learn to say, we've hung up our guilt, I'm doing the best I can, now get off my back.

*Whom do you confide in besides your husband?*
No one.

*Do you have a number of close friends?*
Yes, I have a lot of friends and when I said no one just now I meant I do not discuss very many of the details of my life with anybody except my husband. On the other hand, I have very close women friends and men friends with whom I discuss certain things. But I don't have a sisterly confessor.

*What made you decide to leave a tenured Presidential appointment as federal judge and join the Cabinet to re-shape the Department of Education?*
I thought carefully about the possibility of joining the Cabinet, and I discussed it with my husband. I concluded that a midcareer change would be wonderful. It was an opportunity for an entirely new learning experience. I had been on the bench for eighteen years, and although I learned something new every day, the steepness of the learning curve had definitely gone down. [RISKING LINKING]

*I realize that a root metaphor for you is that life is a mountain and that the fun of it comes only in climbing, and the steeper the better. Has any other situation from the past acted as a metaphor for you?*
Yes. "The past is prologue." Every single thing I have learned before applies now in many ways. After all, human beings are human beings no matter where they are, from Cabinet members to Presidents. On every level, despite differences in personalities and jobs, every single human being needs recognition and support.

*Have you experienced great differences in your own organizational behavior from being a judge, and therefore acting apolitically, to an opposite mode—that of being essentially political?*
My behavior is different because the roles of a Cabinet officer and an appellate judge are different. To be sure, a few of the aspects of the two jobs are similar. For exam-

ple, federal judges testify before Congress on legislation directly affecting the administration of justice in the federal courts. Cabinet officers testify before Congress on many issues, especially on legislation authorizing or funding activities of their departments. Many other phases of these jobs are completely different. For instance, federal judges can take no part in political activities. They cannot participate in any kind of fund-raising, not only for political parties or causes but also for charitable organizations. Without violating the law, no one can try to influence a judge in a pending case, other than the authorized representatives of litigants acting within the strict requirements that regulate communications with the court. In contrast, all kinds of persons and groups can, with propriety, lobby Cabinet officers to try to persuade the officer to support or oppose actions by the Administration, the Department, or Congress, as long as they do not offer any kind of improper inducement.

*What decisions have you made about making living apart from your husband in what's called the bicoastal family?*

It is not a happy situation to be separated from a husband I love very much. But we are working it out as best we can. I can get to California only rarely, but my husband has been able to come to Washington at least briefly every month, and we do manage to meet one another in other cities in which I am speaking. We hope that we can find a way to spend much more time together.

*Looking back, do you have any wish that something else would have happened or you had taken another lead or another path in some way?*

No. As a matter of fact, I consider myself to have had sheer dumb incredible luck to have found myself taking what, retrospectively, turned out to be the right choices at the right times.

# CHAPTER FOURTEEN

# The Parable of the Talents

I remember the Parable of the Talents from the days when the Bible was read in the public schools. In this story a man called his three servants before him and gave them of his goods or talents, each according to his ability. Then he went on a journey and left them to do with their talents as they would. The first and second servants invested their talents and doubled their share, but the third servant was afraid to use his lord's gift and buried it in the earth. After a long time the man returned and asked his servants what they had done with their talents. When he heard from the first two men he was pleased and rewarded them with greater responsibility, but he admonished the third man for hiding his talents and having nothing to show for them.

The successful people interviewed in the preceding chapters serve as models because they have enhanced their careers by developing talent *and* nontechnical skills. And in going beyond their talent, they have contributed immeasurably to their professions. They have demonstrated all six Critical Career Competences as a matter of course, perhaps unaware of the skills they were using.

## The Learn-Do-Teach Cycle

Sometimes one model helps to illuminate another. So first consider the learn-do-teach system. This three-stage system, if followed through with a spirit of commitment, can result in successful careering. We all need to learn new things, to practice and master them, and then to teach them to others. This movement through the complete process of doing something provides us with perspective and understanding, as well as a system for involvement in our work and for personal growth. Without this kind of movement, we stay stuck as perpetual students, or dissatisfied workers, or uninspired teachers. We can't continue to teach unless we ourselves continue to learn. To avoid living like a broken record, we must move through stages of careering and actually recycle ourselves. We must frequently reconsider what we've learned in order to go forward in our present endeavor or begin a wholly new one. Then we need to practice whatever it is that we have set out to learn until we have mastered it. At that point we can pass our experience on to others. The penalty for not moving is that we hinder our potential and limit our ability to change or adapt to a new situation.

## A Developmental Process

Each one of the Six Critical Career Competences is developmental; that is, each one is infinitely expandable. In the most profound sense, we are never finished with any one of them. But we do seem to move on from the first to the second and on to the sixth, in developmental sequence. Some of us will take our whole lives to move once through all of them. Others of us will move through these competences, completing the cycle, and then begin again. This return seems to be on a level more profound than when we started out the first time. With the familiarity that we now have, we can bring a new awareness to our use of the competences. Sometimes we will go back to a competence that we feel needs more attention, more improvement. In the most successful people's lives, this return occurs many times, proving that we all can continue to learn throughout our lives and not only at one particular time. When you consider the lives of the successful people I interview here, you can see that at their ages—in their forties, fifties, and sixties—they are all at new beginnings. Far from thinking about retiring or reflecting back on old accomplishments, they are each at a threshold, about to take a new risk or have an experience they have never had before. They have not stopped wanting to learn and grow.

## Origins

I came to identify the skills for success after a long search. I took the opportunity that a doctoral dissertation provided (*Careering: Identifying Critical Career Competences from Everyday Lawyering;* unpublished dissertation, UCLA, 1976) and set about to find these kinds of skills and categorize them. I didn't have any idea of what they would be or how they would arrange themselves in sets or patterns or systems. I did not act from any already established theory. I decided to interview successful people because I thought they would be most likely to demonstrate these unidentified skills. I wanted them to tell me exactly what they did and not provide accounts or theories of what, in retrospect, they believed about their successful careering. Then I narrowed my focus to lawyers, simply to limit the professional sector I would research and because I thought that they would not be opposed to talking about their career strategies. And talk they did.

From the transcripts of my conversations with them, I mapped their career lives; that is, I actually drew their moves and found patterns in the forty-seven maps hung around my office. First I realized that there were four stages that were a part of the lives of these successful people: early personal development and a strong sense of self in early life; varied experiences in adolescence and young adulthood, including working and learning, and general preparation for adult responsibility; a willingness to explore people and ideas, to take risks; and a strong sense of opportunity for self-expression in many situations. From these four stages I began to work out what are now the six competences which are so critical to successful careering. I drew them out of what the lawyers told me. But I also knew that they had to be congruent with what I had seen in consulting for large organizations and private individuals. I knew that what the Achievers did had to match what the Sustainers did not know how to do or refused to do.

Once I had identified the skills, some interesting patterns emerged. I found that I could divide the six competences into three different spheres—individual, or-

ganizational, and societal—from the most personal level
to the largest, most worldly.

The diagram below demonstrates how the competences relate to each other and to the three spheres. The
skills on the upper line are what I call *internal*, the ones
underneath are *relational*. Experiencing Doing and then
Risking Linking are the initial competences and mostly

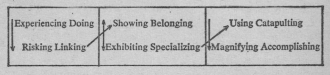

INDIVIDUAL ⟶ ORGANIZATIONAL ⟶ SOCIETAL

involve individual explorations. The next pair, Showing
Belonging and Exhibiting Specializing, are group-related
skills—no matter what the group is, a large corporate setting or a small special committee within a professional
association. Of the three pairs, they are the competences
that above all require group interaction. The last pair,
Using Catapulting and Magnifying Accomplishing, most
particularly relate to an exchange with society in a
larger sense.

To move from an internal competence to a relational
one, from an individual stance to a societal one, means
change. And changing our role anywhere along the path
from beginner to master is truly a change in identity.
To change who we are to ourselves and to others pro-
duces confusion and fear. We feel confused when we
are in the limbo-like state between roles, not knowing
how to act or what to expect. And we feel afraid of both
success and failure because either means new roles, new
goals, new territory, and new relationships once we have
taken another step. However, though there is real anxiety
according to everyone who has experienced successful
careering, there are more than enough rewards. The
greatest is a sense of personal development and contribution, a sense that our lives have a significance that
goes beyond our individual sphere.

This anatomy of successful careering presents the heretofore hidden structure of the system of working and

moving forward, as seen in the lives of a large group of successful people. It is meant to serve as a guide toward making our careers work in more satisfying and fulfilling ways and to stimulate a thoughtful investment of talent and aspiration toward realizing our potential to achieve the greatest possible success in any field.

## ABOUT THE AUTHOR

Adele Scheele is a nationally known career strategist who directs individuals, both privately and in organizations, in taking charge of their working lives and in creating opportunities for themselves and their companies. She received a B.S. from the University of Pennsylvania, an M.A. from California State University at Northridge, and a Ph.D. with honors from UCLA, as a Change Management Fellow. Dr. Scheele frequently appears on network radio and television.

For more information contact:

Dr. Adele Scheele
1722 Westwood Blvd.
Los Angeles, California 90024
213 470-2828

# HELP FOR THE WORKING WOMAN